Diversity Done Right, DEI expert Tyronne Stoudemire emphatically shows that diversity isn't just about having a balanced representation of race and gender in the halls of academia, the cubicles of corporate America, or the legislative halls of Congress. An authentic respect and embracing of diversity begin in the heart. It's something we as leaders strive to have not just to check the box but also because we want our companies and communities to accurately reflect the mosaic that is America (and, quite frankly, the kingdom of God). Diversity entails the beautiful conglomeration of voices, experiences, languages, cultures, ethnicities, and genders that represent all of _us_. _Diversity Done Right_ enhances our collective well-being and the greater good.

~ Dr. Jeanne Porter King
Minister, Author, Leadership Expert,
President of TransPorter Group Inc.

* * *

Whether you are leading others in the workplace or you're a teacher purposed with engaging future leaders in pertinent conversations about the ongoing issues around diversity—what's working, what's not working, and what seems irrevocably broken—add this book to your repertoire. It is an engaging, thought-provoking read filled with current stats, real-life situations, and personal experiences showing why learning to be comfortable in a global family is important.

~ Andrew Young
Former U.S. Ambassador to the United Nations
Activist, Civil Servant

* * *

For decades, I've watched with great pride how Tyronne Stoudemire has carried the torch of great civil rights leaders and community organizers like Dr. Martin Luther King Jr., Bishop Arthur M. Brazier, and Bishop

Endorsements for *Diversity Done Ri*

In the aftermath of tragedies like the murder of George l
hanging of Sandra Bland, and the shoot-first, ask-questions-la
of many black men and women at the hands of officers of the law
Done Right is right on time. While it focuses on the impact o
diversity primarily in the workplace, when we get to the ro
corporations need DEI experts on the payroll in the twenty-firs
the reason is not much different than the reason men and wc
Floyd, Bland, Breonna Taylor, and Philando Castile lost their li
hands of police officers who couldn't see beyond the color of t

~ Be

Civil Rights

* * *

Over 60 years ago, the Reverend Dr. Martin Luther King stoo
steps of the Lincoln Memorial and delivered his iconic "I Have a
speech. Part of his dream? That one day, his children would be
not by the color of their skin but by the content of their charac
country has made some strides since then, to be sure. Howevei
legalized barriers once kept marginalized groups on the outs
achieving anything remotely close to the American dream, the
been replaced with something much more subtle and dan;
Implicit bias impacts every facet of life. In this essential book, \
by one of our nation's foremost voices on diversity, equity, and incl
Tyronne Stoudemire shows how implicit bias can erode diversity e
particularly in corporate America, and how we can overcome it. *Di*
Done Right sounds the trumpet on diversity today and is a must-re
leaders and those they lead.

~ Xernona Cl:

Civil Rights Advocate, Assistant to Rev. Dr. Martin Luther Ki:

* * *

Lawrence James London into the exclusive spaces of corporate America. Because of his leadership, creativity, and passion for DEI issues, wherever Tyronne lands, he makes those companies forerunners in fostering authentic diversity, not the kind that gives just enough. That's one reason we awarded him the MLK PUSH for Excellence Award. As a civil rights leader who has leaned into Tyronne's expertise and worked alongside him at PUSH, I am excited that corporate leaders, DEI officers in training, emerging community leaders and activists, and those who have been trying to break their way through that proverbial glass ceiling get to learn from my friend by way of this book. *Diversity Done Right*, which is so needed for our times, stresses that true diversity goes way beyond affirmative action. The purpose of achieving diversity, equity, and inclusion, particularly in our workplaces isn't to pacify those victimized by perpetuated bias but to rectify the sins of America's founding fathers.

~ Rev. Jesse L. Jackson, Rainbow PUSH Coalition

* * *

I am thrilled to endorse Tyronne Stoudemire's groundbreaking work, *Diversity Done Right*. As the pastor of a mega-church in an urban community, I understand the importance of embracing diversity among leadership within our congregation and beyond. Tyronne, a leading DEI practitioner and one of our dedicated deacons, has not only understood this message but has taken it to new heights with his insightful and transformative book. He draws from his own experiences and expertise to provide a comprehensive guide to navigating the complexities of diversity in today's world and developing a deep understanding of the principles that underpin true inclusion.

~ Dr. Byron T. Brazier
Pastor, Apostolic Church of God

* * *

Diversity Done Right is a must-have for every organization to see real-world examples and tools to achieve proven results for global DEI. Drawing on his decades of experience, Tyronne Stoudemire gives the reader strategies and solutions for impactful and systemic change.

~ Dr. Sheila Robinson
Chief Publishing Executive

* * *

Tyronne's rare blend of candor, courage, and competence has positioned him globally as a true leader among leaders in the space of diversity, equity, and inclusion. Many people talk the talk, but Tyronne walks the walk and points the way forward in *Diversity Done Right*. In this book, Tyronne combines moving stories from the battlefield with timeless insights to challenge us all to be better and do better, one act of kindness at a time.

~ Dr. Nicholas Pearce, Clinical Professor of Management &
Organizations, Northwestern University
Kellogg School of Management

* * *

Although *Diversity Done Right* is directed at business and corporate settings, it is of relevance to anyone who works, lives, and worships in multicultural environments. It is of great help to policymakers as well as those of us who want to be in good relationship with coworkers and neighbors. Tyronne has described a path to understanding the complexities of crossing from one culture to the next. In many situations, we may be hesitant, knowing that our lack of understanding may lead to offensive statements, behaviors, policies, and situations that disadvantage those of other cultures. These actions are often inadvertent. Yet they have considerable potential to be disruptive or even destructive to collaborations and relationships.

I have had many conversations with Tyronne about the issues discussed in this book. I am glad to see it in writing so that his wisdom will be available to all. He brings to bear his experience as Senior Vice President of Diversity and Inclusion at Hyatt Corporation, a global company whose livelihood is hospitality, and requires all employees to understand how to welcome people of diverse backgrounds. Tyronne's experience crosses North and South America, Europe, Asia, the Middle East, and Africa, giving him a broad perspective of how cultures can clash. In this book, he draws together his professional and personal experience with theory, data, and studies demonstrating the impact of cultural divides. His understanding of the cultures of the corporate world gives him many examples of how cultural misunderstanding impedes success. He challenges us to be skeptical of generalizations, and to be aware of our own biases, which may be entirely unconscious. He calls us to examine what we have been told, and may even believe, beliefs that can create misunderstandings and even offense in our relationships with those of other cultures. His insights are thought provoking and enlightening. Furthermore, he delves into social and psychological factors that contribute to cultural inequities, as well as power dynamics that encourage the powerful to maintain the status quo. The "Done Right" is a call to dig deeper, to not be satisfied with superficial diversity efforts, but to thoughtfully examine how to successfully address our differences.

I am grateful to Tyronne for the insights that he has given me in our conversations over the years. As you read this book, I pray that his knowledge and insight will be a blessing to you the reader, to your work and to your relationships.

~ Therese J McGee, PhD, Licensed Clinical Psychologist

* * *

This book is a must-have for every organization to see real-world examples and tools to achieve proven results for global DEI. Drawing on his decades of experience Tyronne Stoudemire gives the reader strategies and solutions for impactful and systemic change.

~ Dr. Sheila Robinson
Publisher & CEO

Tyronne is *the* person to follow regarding DEIA in the corporate world. His depth of experience, and ability to read an organization's culture to identify access points to greater inclusivity is exemplary. More than that, his open heart and deep love for humanity is expressed in every page. A must read for anyone in the business.

~ Leslie Traub, Former Partner, Cook Ross Inc

NAVIGATING CULTURAL DIFFERENCE TO CREATE

diversity

POSITIVE CHANGE IN THE WORKPLACE

done

right

Tyronne Stoudemire

WILEY

For general information on our other products and services or for technical support, please contact our Customer Care Department within the United States at (800) 762-2974, outside the United States at (317) 572-3993 or fax (317) 572-4002.

Wiley also publishes its books in a variety of electronic formats. Some content that appears in print may not be available in electronic formats. For more information about Wiley products, visit our web site at www.wiley.com.

Library of Congress Cataloging-in-Publication Data is Available:

ISBN 9781394228515 (Cloth)
ISBN 9781394230723 (ePub)
ISBN 9781394230709 (ePDF)

Cover Design: Wiley
Cover Image: © mazaya /Adobe Stock
Author Photo: Courtesy of the Author

SKY10069362_031124

I dedicate this book to my parents,
Edgar and Carolyn Stoudemire,
my wife, Valerie, and daughter, Kennedy,
my in-laws, Van and Zenobia Newell,
Bishop Arthur M. Brazier and Isabel Brazier,
and Bishop Lawrence J. London.

Contents

Acknowledgments

This book has been in the making for many years and during those years I have been touched by the courage, insights, generosity, and compassion of many mentors and teachers. I would like to acknowledge and thank you all for providing me with a safe place to learn and share and for modeling excellence in all that you do.

My circle of mentors and teachers includes John W. Rogers, Jr., founder, chairman, and co-CEO of Ariel Investments, one of the largest Black-owned global asset management firms. John sits on the corporate boards of The Times, Exelon, and Nike, and serves as a trustee to the University of Chicago. Additionally, he is chairman of the Chicago Urban League. Mellody Hobson, another mentor, is president and co-CEO of Ariel Investments and the chairwoman of Starbucks Corporation. She also sits on the board of JPMorgan Chase and was chairwoman of DreamWorks, board until its sale to Comcast. My teacher and mentor, the Reverend Jesse Jackson, is a civil rights activist and current president of Operation Push. Mrs. Xernona Clayton Brady, an American civil rights leader and broadcasting executive, is also a part of my mentoring circle. During the Civil Rights Movement, she worked for the National Urban League and Southern Christian Leadership Conference, where she became involved in the work of Dr. Martin Luther King, Jr. Xernona Clayton Brady created the Trumpet Awards, a program dedicated to honoring African American achievement in the arts, science, and politics. Another mentor of mine is James H. Lowry, a business icon, strategic advisor, and nationally recognized pioneer and advocate for minority economic development. Lowry was the first

African American consultant for McKinsey & Company. He later headed his own successful consulting firm for many years prior to becoming the first African American senior partner at the prestigious Boston Consulting Group. Bishop Lawrence J. London, pastor of the New Jerusalem Missionary Baptist Church in Detroit, Michigan, for 50 years, and Bishop Arthur M. Brazier, activist and author, were also great mentors to me. Bishop Brazier pastored for many decades for the Apostolic Church of God in Chicago, one of the mega churches in this city. My mentor and dear friend, Juanita Brown, has been a stable force in my life. Her spiritual guidance and courageous allyship in the workplace is unparalleled. When it was unpopular, she started one of the first Employee Resource Groups at one of my employers. She took it from an underground meet-up, that provided a safe space for Black employees, to a shining example applauded by our executives and modeled at other corporations.

I appreciate your love, care, time, and wisdom, and that all of you subscribe to the philosophy "Each one, teach one." You helped to shape my worldview. My interactions with you were my first introduction to "empathy and compassion."

About the Author

Tyronne Stoudemire was born in Detroit, Michigan, and was raised just blocks away from Motown's Hitsville U.S.A. In 1970, his family moved to a predominately White suburb of Detroit. At a very young age, Tyronne had to learn how to navigate through cultural differences being the only Black child in the classroom. His classmates would often mistake him as having Indian heritage and would yell, "Go back to India!" His strong faith and compassion for others helped him to navigate through his adversities. At 24, he moved to Chicago and became an active member of the Apostolic Church of God.

Tyronne's professional career spans over 35 years. He is an internationally recognized executive and speaker, experienced in advancing diversity, equity, and inclusion. He has worked and traveled extensively in several countries outside of the United States. Examples of his leadership roles include: Senior VP of Global Diversity, Equity, and Inclusion at Hyatt Hotel Corporation; Principal, Diversity & Inclusion Consulting at Mercer Consulting; Global Head of Community, Diversity & Inclusion at Aon Hewitt; and Executive Leadership Council Member and Chairman of the Board for Black Ensemble Theater.

Tyronne has been featured in countless publications and has received numerous awards for his work. He was named one of the Top Executives in Diversity by *Crains* Chicago and *Black Enterprise* magazine; and honored as one of the 50 Diversity Champions by *Diversity Woman* magazine. Tyronne is also the recipient of *Who's Who in Black Chicago: The Inaugural Edition*, Thurgood Marshall College Fund of Excellence Award, Most Influential African American People Voice, Push for

Excellence Award (Dr. Martin Luther King Jr. Celebration and Scholarship Breakfast), among several other awards.

Tyronne has been nicknamed "Mr. Red Carpet," as his networks and ability to command a seat at the table are unrivaled. The connection with and advisor role during Barack Obama's successful presidential campaign are particularly notable. He has also collaborated and worked side-by-side with other history makers including being a senior adviser to Illinois governor Pat Quinn, and Chicago mayors Richard M. Daley and Rahm Emmanuel.

Tyronne and his wife, Valerie, have one daughter, Kennedy, and are engaged in many community programs and their church.

1

Introduction and Overview

Why This Book Was Written

Polarization and conflict across and within groups is often rooted in misunderstandings, miscommunication, bias, and the collision of different worldviews. These cognitive and social drivers lead to mistrust and behaviors that would shock and surprise many. Examples of interactions in which individuals are offended or harmed verbally or physically have been pervasive in the media. Yet those unaffected often question their veracity.

This book will shine a light on group dynamics (organizational and societal) that contribute to polarization and the erosion of cross-cultural interactions. I will leverage the power of storytelling with the intent to appeal to both your head and your heart. While many readers may be dismayed with the sobering reality that surrounds interactions across demographic groups, it is my intent to raise general awareness and provide tools that individuals and organizations can use to move forward.

I am writing this book in 2023. This time is one in which it seems America can barely catch its breath. The changes our society has been and lived through in the last five years have been exhausting. We have experienced a pandemic, staggering changes in legislation, natural disasters including wildfires and destructive hurricanes, global warming, and other destabilizing events. One might think that many of these horrific and unpredicted events would unite us as a people, as a society. They have, to some extent as we search for applicable remedies. But during this same time, we have heard of just as many inhumane acts perpetrated by individuals. There have been mass shootings (almost daily), hate-based assaults, and xenophobic reactions to immigration policies.

While there appear to be a proliferation of incidents that cause divisiveness within society and within organizations, many of these are rebirths of issues from the past. They are more prevalent now given the almost real-time exposure we have via social media. Would we even know about the murder of George Floyd had it not been recorded on the cell phone of a 17-year-old female African American, our Rosa Parks of today. This technology was not available to capture the many lynchings, human trafficking, and hate crimes from the past—crimes like the despicable torture and murder of Emmett Till. And for every Emmett Till, there are probably numerous others whose stories were never told. On the one hand, our survival and push for social justice after these events speaks to the strength of the human spirit. On the other hand, the fear and hatred that motivates these tragic acts speaks to our civilization's frailty and opportunity to grow.

I am highlighting these egregious acts and violation of human rights within our society for their shock value. Yes, I said it—*for* their shock value—as I believe, as Benjamin Franklin so vehemently expressed, *"Justice will not be served until those who are unaffected are as outraged as those who are."* For many, these acts are not shocking; for those to whom they are, my goal is to raise awareness, stir emotions, and sound the trumpet for empathy and action. This, in my experience, is the critical pathway for change. Our capacity to advocate for social justice has implications for the workplace. We spend one-third of our lives in the workplace, and what happens outside of it has a significant impact on the state of mind we bring to work.

We need courageous and competent champions in both the public and corporate domain to speak out against social injustices and leverage their resources and their base to create change. We can reflect upon and take a lesson from the many champions that came forward over the course of our nation's history. As an example, this year (2023) marks the 60-year anniversary of the March on Washington, in which more than a quarter million individuals, from all races and ethnicities, flocked to the nation's capital to take a stand for jobs and freedom. There they witnessed the Reverend Dr. Martin Luther King, Jr. making his famous "I have a Dream" speech. Dr. King was a pivotal champion of civil rights, but not the first and certainly not the last. "Harriet Tubman led so that Rosa Parks could sit, so that Martin Luther could walk, so that Barack Obama could run, and so that Ketanji Brown Jackson could rule."

About Me

My hope is that you as a reader will benefit from the blended, inclusive, and diverse background that I bring to this book. As a senior executive, I can share my insights on the conversations and expectations of leadership as well as the hurdles I have had to navigate to make it to this echelon. As a diversity, equity, and inclusion practitioner, I have become well entrenched in identifying and applying numerous frameworks, strategies, and tools that have had an impact in shaping an organization's culture into one that is inclusive, promotes equity, and values continuous improvement. I have leveraged this skill, along with my insights and strategic networks, to reengineer and turn around underperforming business units and organizations within the space of diversity, equity, and inclusion.

I have over 30 years of professional experience and am recognized internationally for advancing diversity, equity, and inclusion. In the course of my work, I have traveled extensively in several countries, giving me the opportunity to immerse myself in cultures different than the United States. I've noticed where there are stark differences in expectations and customs, and where we align. In every country I've traveled to, I've noted leading practices we can glean from as well as opportunities for growth. I am humbled by how vast our world is and that there's always something new to learn.

I was given the nickname "Mr. Red Carpet" by a colleague as I have grown an expansive network and run into people whom I know, or who know me. Everywhere I go, many have asked, "Who are you?" and "How do you know so many people?" This has enabled me access to many exclusive venues. I say all of this not to brag, but to share that I did not grow up with the privilege that many of my White colleagues have. I have earned a seat at the table through my competence, my diligence in nurturing relationships, by being authentic, by demonstrating curiosity, and through a willingness to learn from those with a different point of view. I believe it's the power of our worldviews that shapes our beliefs and our behaviors.

I mention my vast circle of mentors and teachers in the Acknowledgments section of this book, where I honor their positions and accomplishments. This group includes John W. Rogers, Jr., Mellody Hobson, Reverend Jesse Jackson, Mrs. Xernona Clayton Brady, James H. Lowry, Bishop Lawrence J. London, Bishop Arthur M. Brazier, and Juanita Brown. The list of individuals only scratches the surface of those who have influenced my life positively. I appreciate their love, care, time, and wisdom, and that all these individuals subscribed to the philosophy "Each one, teach one." These relationships introduced me to, and reinforced for me, the impact of demonstrating compassion.

I am a family man. My wife and daughter (a recent college graduate from HBCU Hampton University) are my motivation for getting up every morning and navigating the unstable waters of corporate America. They are also my anchors and they keep me grounded, lest I get too intoxicated by all my accomplishments. And trust me, we all need these anchors.

I have been very active in the community and have sat on and led many nonprofit boards, including the Chicago Urban League and chairman of the board for the Black Ensemble Theater. My values align with the vision and mission of the community organizations in which I participate. These missions range from advocating for arts and culture to eradicating systemic racism.

As a Black man living in America, I can share my more than 60 years of lived experience in a historically marginalized group and all the rage, fear, hope, and joy that comes with that. Although I currently reside in Chicago, I was born and raised in Detroit, just blocks away from Motown's Hitsville U.S.A. Detroit is famous for its distinctive Motown music sound from the 1960s. Long known as the automobile capital of the world, Detroit is home to a rich mix of people from various ethnic backgrounds, including citizens of Italian, English, German, Polish, Irish, Mexican, Middle Eastern, African, and Greek descent.

At a very young age I had to learn how to navigate through cultural differences, being the only Black child in the classroom of all White teachers and students. My classmates often mistook me as having Indian heritage and would constantly taunt me, yelling "Go back to India!" The largest single immigrant group in metro Detroit comes from India. Of the 41,000 people of Indian heritage living in the region's four main counties, about half live in Oakland County, with 11,000 in Wayne County and the rest in Macomb and Washtenaw counties.

As an adult, I have also experienced microaggressions and blatant offenses as many of us have. What I believe is more notable is that my deep faith, perseverance, and capacity to employ self-empowerment strategies has enabled me to advance to the highest levels in both the corporate sector and in the community.

My pathway to leadership was not a traditional one and I will expand on this in later chapters. I have experienced both the highs and the lows associated with being an executive, from enjoying VIP access when flying and staying at five-star luxury hotels privileges to being racially targeted while simply driving, walking, or sitting still minding my own business. From all my experiences I have gained wisdom, empathy, and insights I hope to pass on to those of you reading this book.

Teachable Moments

As a diversity, equity, and inclusion (DEI) practitioner, I regularly share stories and examples that can be leveraged as teachable moments. For example, in my role as adjunct faculty at Northwestern University's Kellogg School of Management, I created an experiment to demonstrate how bias manifests. I asked one Black student and one White student to walk down Michigan Avenue in Chicago with a cane and dark glasses to represent someone who is visually impaired. They were asked to do so in a manner that would suggest they might need help and were at risk of possibly harming themselves. What we discovered from this exercise was that the majority of bystanders who were willing to help did so for the White student. These bystanders were both White and people of color. Far less support was given to the Black student. In fact, the Black student, pretending to be blind, was often treated aggressively. People would nudge and push him to the side and make demeaning remarks to suggest that he was trying to take advantage of others or faking his blindness. The students in my class were quite surprised at this discrepancy.

This experiment is just one of many scenarios that help create "Ah Ha" moments of the manifestation of bias. I am a strong believer that Ah Ha or "Light Bulb" moments are the fuel for behavior and systemic change. A favorite framework of mine that I share with leaders is that Ah Ha moments and feedback lead to self-correction, which leads to the ability to influence others and subsequently the ability to influence systems (see Figure 1.1).

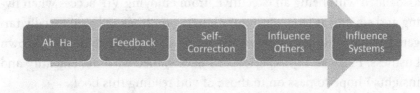

FIGURE 1.1   "Ah Ha" moments framework.

I will speak more about how I have observed this phenomenon and leveraged this framework in various chapters of this book.

Target Audiences and How You Will Benefit

The intended audience for this book is varied. For leaders of organizations and other influencers within the community, it provides a framework for looking at DEI and understanding individual and group dynamics that drive hostile and/or discriminatory behaviors. Additionally, this book will provide leaders with tested approaches and tools for creating change.

For individuals who come from a privileged background, this book will provide a glance into some of the egregious behaviors that are often supported systemically. I will offer an interpretation of these behaviors through the lenses of diversity, equity, inclusion, neuroscience, history, and social psychology. I will speak about allyship and the role you can play in advancing equity and inclusion.

For individuals from marginalized groups, this book speaks to the reality you may very well know and experience and provides insightful approaches for self-empowerment.

Additionally, this book will provide relevant cases, theories, and applications useful within academia.

How This Book Is Structured

Each chapter will focus on a different topic relevant to inclusion and equity. I will share my experiences and the stories of others to highlight how outlandish behaviors are pervasive despite the advances we have made in the corporate and public sectors. In fact, we are seeing a trend toward reversing civil rights and social justice progress through legislation, policy reform, and organized efforts like the January 6, 2021, insurrection at the U.S. Capitol. These events highlight the desire by those with historical power and privilege to turn back to the "good ole days." To this end I will highlight historical milestones related to equity and inclusion as well as historical adversities. I am a strong believer that if we don't know our history, we are doomed to repeat it.

Well-known frameworks and tools for assessing, developing, and demonstrating cross-cultural competence and humility will be presented and integrated into each chapter. The objective of each chapter is to provoke thought, spark courageous and informed conversations, as well as to inspire action that creates impact.

In **Chapter 2, Say It Isn't So: How Bias Overrides Evidence**, I will cover the topic of bias and how our biases, both conscious and unconscious, override the evidence that is often right in front of us. As humans, we all have bias. If you have a brain, you have bias. Our biases can be a protective mechanism, but they can also lead to decisions and actions that harm and exclude others. Understanding our biases is the first step for managing them and changing our behaviors. I say it is a first step, because our inner child will go kicking and screaming to avoid change. While an oxymoron, it's often said that there are only two things people dislike: the way things are—and change; or, as DEI guru Dr. Mary-Frances Winters says it best, "only wet babies like change!"[1]

In this chapter I will also talk about systemic bias—how bias is embedded in our institutions and other macro systems. This type of bias has serious implications for a marginalized group's ability to make advances within society and to experience equitable outcomes. Systemic bias colludes with other isms—systemic racism, systemic sexism, systemic ableism. Take your pick.

Along with societal illustrations, I will share examples in this chapter of how bias manifests in the workplace, primarily in the talent acquisition, management, and development space.

In **Chapter 3, Will vs. Skill**, I will juxtapose intentions against impact, or will against skill and how this can either thwart or facilitate efforts to create equitable and inclusive workplaces. In a nutshell there are many individuals who perceive their intentions as commendable, yet the results are formidable. What is missing in the equation is often the skill, competency, or awareness needed to explore situations through a new lens and apply strategic solutions.

This chapter will address the benefit that organizations can gain by expanding their partnerships to engage individuals and groups with different life experiences and the professional expertise needed to identify new solutions. This requires organizations to move beyond being insular to being curious enough to explore new approaches. In my experience, this is where transformative change can begin.

Too many of us have missed an opportunity to take a stand when we have seen an injustice. **Chapter 4, Did You See Something? Bystanders and Allies**, covers the behavior of bystanders. What most readily comes to mind when we think of bystanders are incidents captured on the news of individuals standing by or walking past an individual they see being assaulted. Others are using their phones to at least capture what is happening but nonetheless staying clear of the incident. It also occurs in the workplace in meetings where coworkers witness others being subjected to micro-inequities, but neither say nor do anything to support those impacted. What is beneath this behavior? Does it boil down to cowardice vs. courage, apathy vs. empathy? I will share my perspective on why this behavior occurs but will move past this to advocate ways in which we can play a more supportive role as we view and observe offenses.

Chapter 5, The Many Faces of Power and Privilage, will be a discourse on how power and privilege manifest. Power, as a construct, is neutral. It is simply energy directed toward something. How power dynamics play out amongst different groups can make it either a deterrent or facilitator. Those who have power typically have the ability to provide or take away resources, to reward or penalize others; and so, holding on to power becomes a survival strategy of sorts.

Privilege is often the companion to power. Groups who are privileged are typically born into benefits that they did not earn. Individuals within these groups feel an entitlement to have certain things, to experience life in a certain way that does not disturb this entitlement. Recently, the media has given the nickname Karen to those who abuse their privilege, following the incident of a White woman calling the police on a Black man who was simply bird-watching in New York City's Central Park. In Chapter 5, I will also talk about how power and privilege are contextual. Depending on the situation, we may have it or not. Finally, I will share my insights on how leaders can use their power to empower others.

In **Chapter 6, Stereotypes**, I will revisit how and why stereotypes persist. Stereotypes have an evolutionary component to them and are often based on historical incidents. Stereotypes differ from archetypes in that stereotypes suggest that all members from a demographic group will have similar characteristics or behaviors. Archetypes suggest a characteristic or behavior is observable within a group as a general tendency, but that every individual within that group does not necessarily portray it. Most stereotypes are negative and contribute to the emotions, fears, and biases we have toward certain individuals and groups.

Within this chapter I will refer to specific research on the impact of stereotypes, including those held for Asian Americans. As an example, since the 1960s, Asian Americans have been depicted as the United States' "model minority," largely due to significant increases in their mobility attributable to their educational attainment and success. While on the surface this may sound like a vantage point, it is in reality a double-edged sword. Research indicates that while Asians may be viewed as high on competence and intelligence, they are simultaneously stereotyped as low on social skills (e.g., nerdy, antisocial, nonassertive). The buy-in to this narrative has contributed to the underrepresentation of Asian Americans in leadership roles, also known as the "Bamboo Ceiling." I will expand on related adverse outcomes of stereotypes in this chapter and recommend frameworks that help raise awareness and dismantle stereotypes, separating myths from reality.

Chapter 7, Be Like Us: Adapting to Organizational Culture, builds on previous chapters and addresses how perceived stereotypes, bias, and rigid organizational cultures lead to assimilation. Assimilation can be thought of as the process in which individuals from marginalized groups are encouraged to assume the behaviors, values, norms, and beliefs of the dominant group. Organizations often sanction assimilation but use acculturation as a more sanitized term for it. I will talk about how individuals in underrepresented groups will consent to assimilation by minimizing their authentic identities. This includes a range of actions including changing one's name, appearance, communication style, and behaviors. This is often a strategy of going along to get along, trying to "fit" in; but there is a cost to living disingenuously. It can be exhausting to shove your authentic self into the "closet"; and research indicates that this has impacts on productivity and engagement.

There is a saying that "culture eats strategy for breakfast." So, despite the detailed strategic plans organizations put in place to address diversity, equity, and inclusion, if this is not accompanied by taking a close look at the culture and the impact on employees, efforts will not be sustained.

Finally, in **Chapter 8, Change Starts With You**, I will review some of my favorite frameworks and activities that practitioners and organizational leaders can reference as they embark on their journeys to create more empathetic and inclusive work environments. In my work, I have found that introducing frameworks, such as "change starts with you," or "demonstrating empathy and compassion," provide a beacon or guidepost for employees and leaders. Models like the "seven dimensions of culture" developed by Trompenaars and Hamden-Turner,[2] the "six dimensions of culture" developed by Hofstede,[3] and the "Developmental Model of Intercultural Sensitivity" developed by Bennet[4,5] will be described. Frameworks provide us with a common language to understand our behaviors and actions and to gauge where we are making progress or where further improvements are needed. These frameworks have been invaluable in the conversations I have held with other leaders, when I am keynoting within a conference stadium of thousands, and in my personal interactions outside of work.

So, buckle your seat belts and join me as we embark upon an odyssey of discovery and reflection. At this altitude we will experience turbulence but, not to worry, even turbulence can become comfortable once you realize it is an unavoidable pathway to reach a new destination . . . and we should always be reaching for new destinations!

2

Say It Isn't So: How Bias Overrides Evidence

Welcome to the Bias Zone

It is a beautiful, sunny day. I am driving to work, about 40 miles from my Chicago residence in Hyde Park, a beautiful neighborhood that embodies the feel of a "small town" in the big city. Hyde Park is well-known for being the home to President Barack Obama, First Lady Michelle Obama, and their family. It also boasts beautiful architecture, a popular science museum, great restaurants, and much more. My office was in the northern suburbs, a global provider of human capital and management consulting services. It operated 500 offices in 120 countries providing consulting, outsourcing, and insurance brokerage services. Its headquarters were in Lincolnshire, Illinois, next to Lake Forest, a wealthy Chicago suburb, and one of the richest cities in the world.

As I am driving, I look to my right and see the border of lush and beautiful green trees with houses peeking through. I look to my left and see other cars racing along the Edens Expressway with drivers focused on getting to their destinations, as am I. Not a care in the world . . . well, not at this point.

I get off on my exit, and suddenly I enter into the "Bias Zone."

Immediately my senses are heightened because someone is following me. What did I do? What could be happening? Lights begin flashing on top of the car behind me, and simultaneously I hear through a speaker, "Pull over" . . . As you might guess, what is taking place has nothing to do with the speed I am driving, the lane I am driving in, or whether or not my taillight is busted. It has everything to do with "driving while Black."

There have been numerous accounts of horrific incidents that have occurred where Black men and women, in particular, have had run-ins with law enforcement that ended very badly, that ended fatally. We can reflect on Rodney King, George Floyd, Tyre Nichols, and numerous others.

Black and brown men have been pulled over more than any other demographic. In the largest study of alleged racial profiling during traffic stops, led by Stanford University, it was found that Blacks are pulled over more frequently than Whites, however they are much less likely to be stopped after sunset, when "a veil of darkness"[1] masks their race. That is one of several examples of systemic bias that emerged from Stanford's five-year study that analyzed 95 million traffic stop records between 2011 to 2018.

The Stanford-led study also found that when drivers were pulled over, officers searched the cars of Blacks and Hispanics more often than Whites. The researchers examined a subset of data from Washington and Colorado, two states that legalized marijuana, and found that while this change resulted in fewer searches overall, and thus fewer searches of Blacks and Hispanics, minorities were still more likely than Whites to have their cars searched after being pulled over.

While this might be hard to believe and grasp for some, it is very believable from my worldview; in fact it is something for which I was primed for years before I was even eligible to drive.

Build in Time to Get Pulled Over

To better examine how bias overrides evidence, let's look more closely at the experience of "driving while Black."

Early Lessons: Driving While Black, 10 and 2

"Driving while Black (DWB), 10 and 2" is "The Talk" that Black parents have with their children, particularly their sons, about how they should behave if they encounter the police. It is a tough and depressing talk. The stakes are really high. Every Black child's parent knows it from when their parent wrapped them in the coarse blanket of love and sat them down for "The Talk."

I remember having "The Talk" with my parents. My parents told my two older brothers and me that if we ever got stopped by the police, make sure you hear and understand their instructions. Have your driver's license and registration within easy reach. Respond with "Yes, sir" or "Yes, ma'am." Keep your hands on the steering wheel at 10 and 2 o'clock. And turn the music off! All of these instructions for ways to behave were not covered at all in driver's ed. I was taught these rules of the road at home, at eight years old. I was still playing with toy trucks and cars at the time!

With no context or constructs for why I should follow these rules, I nonetheless accepted these messages as part of my norm. I then shared these same rules of behavior with my daughter when she approached driving age. It became a filter through which I moved through the world as a youth, and I took it into adulthood. I soon came to experience first-hand, regular encounters with law enforcement, being stopped and pulled over, particularly while driving to work. This often made me late, not to mention, arriving at work in a flustered state of mind.

Empathy or Lack of

What added insult to injury was the lack of empathy I received from my White coworkers who mostly believed I was making this all up. Allow me to back up a bit and provide more context. I'm typically the only Black male in a predominantly White male or female work environment. I often felt that I was not understood and that my contribution was not viewed as valid, that I was unrelatable, that my White colleagues couldn't see what I was seeing. The other thing that I noticed is that many of the individuals were very private about what might be going on outside of work. I, on the other hand, viewed myself as being very extroverted. And one thing about extroverts is that we often talk as we are thinking; and often express what we are feeling. I also wanted people to understand me in a holistic sense so I would talk about what I was doing outside of work. I am involved in many activities in the community where I am helping to lead or advocate.

However, when I was sharing my thoughts, my feelings, and my emotions, it appeared that this was misinterpreted as a lack of professionalism, competency, or problem-solving skills. For example, sharing how I was stopped on the way to work and how this impacted me was viewed by many of my coworkers as an excuse for being late. Because they didn't have the same experiences that I had, they felt I had to be lying or greatly exaggerating the situation! I relayed how I was repeatedly pulled over by the police and interrogated. "Who are you? Why are you here? Whose car are you driving? How long will you be here?"

Their response was, "Well, that's just an excuse. And you've had this excuse now several times." Since my experience and credibility were being questioned, I then had to figure out a strategy. Bottom line, I decided to leave super early to get to work on time, knowing that I was going to get pulled over. Secondly, I stopped sharing this experience, because it was unbelievable to my coworkers. It wasn't believable because it had never happened to them. They could not empathize or sympathize.

Demonstrating Empathy and Compassion

Of the many examples I could share of being pulled over, the one that is most memorable and ultimately had the most impact on me and others unfolded as follows. I remember being invited to my CEO's house for a barbecue. He lived in Lake Forest, an upper-class suburb along the north shore of Chicago. It was on a Saturday afternoon. I got ready to make the hour drive and discovered I didn't have my wallet. I remembered I left it on my desk at the office on Friday! "Oh, my goodness!"

So, knowing that the office was somewhat on the route to the barbecue, my plan was to drive out early, stop at the office, pick up my wallet, which had my license in it, and then head to my CEO's house. The entire route I am thinking "drive right at the speed limit; watch what I am doing." I am praying the whole way!

Well, I made it to my exit, but there was a certain part once I started getting closer to our office campus that I noticed police vehicles following me. "Just let me get to the office!" And I do make it to the office parking lot, but to my dismay I discover that seven or eight squad cars are pulling in at the same time. Darn it! So, there I was surrounded by a brigade of police officers asking me to get out of the car. With all of the activity, an onlooker might have thought the world's most wanted fugitive had been cornered.

I get out of the car and explain right away that I don't have my license. "My wallet is on my desk. Here's my work ID with my photo on it. Please allow me to go in there and come in with me so I can show you my license. I know my driver's license number, so you can verify that I am who I say I am."

You might be surprised that I had memorized my driver's license number. But that is part of the strategy. The police can then check their systems to make a determination and validate your image, your address, your birth date, any outstanding warrants, and other things related to your identity. I had my insurance card. I had my AAA card, my Mercedes Benz card. All these had my name and address on them.

But all of this was not enough or even a consideration for me. I ended up face down on the hood of the car, handcuffed, and swiftly taken to jail. You can't prove who you are. You go to jail. And I have no doubt that no allowances or exceptions were made for me—because I was a Black man in a White community, alleging to work at the global headquarters of a premier consulting firm.

So, we went to the local police station. I know my rights. I get one call. The person I called was the CEO of our company, whose house I was trying to get to for the barbecue. And fortunately for me, he left his house and guests, came to the station, and bailed me out.

That was my first introduction to "demonstrated empathy." I had engaged in many conversations with our CEO and so I was close enough to him for him to know, understand, and trust me. I was part of the company's family. He was empathetic enough to either put himself in my shoes or at least care enough to want to assist and support me. He took action. He left his party and came to the police station to post bail for me, and this translated into an act of compassion.

The Aftermath

When I returned to the office that following week and relayed my story to a Black female coworker, I found out that she had been pulled over because an officer said she was speeding. After running her driver's license, he told her she was driving on a suspended license. Following some discussion, she realized her license was suspended because of unpaid parking tickets her son had on her car. When she explained that to the officer, she was arrested and roughly handled. The officer hand-cuffed her behind her back, pushed her into the backseat of the squad car, and took her off to jail. After being marched through the front door of the police station, she was fingerprinted, required to take a mug shot, and held in a locked holding room until a relative could pick her up. The ironic thing . . . she was never issued a speeding ticket!

We heard that other Black employees were also getting pulled over. So, we began collecting these stories and shared them with our CEO. He was both surprised and furious. A communication went out to the local police department giving the community a stern warning. "If you do not stop harassing our Black associates, we will pull our business out of this community!" This was significant as the company was a major employer and had a globally recognized brand. The economic impact for the com-munity and neighboring communities would have been crippling.

The community and our company agreed to have the entire police department engage in dialogue, training, and assessments of their cross-cultural competency. We were seeking to influence and drive change at the systemic level in which it operated. The encounters between the police force and Black employees at our company were used as teachable moments. We sought to raise awareness of the influence of bias and to create a relationship that would lead to more empathy and changed behaviors.

The Impact

So, it is probable that the business and economic implications for the community drove the decision to do something. Did this bother me? Did I feel personally compensated for having to experience these threatening and humiliating acts? I could have been angry. I could have escalated my experience to the media. I would have been able to garner plenty of support from faith-based and social justice–driven groups within the community. This was during a time in Chicago's history where Operation Push, led by the Reverend Jesse Jackson, and whose board I was on at the time, was very active in publicly challenging businesses to "do the right thing." But I figured that many of the police officers were driven by biases they didn't completely understand, and that dialogue was the better way to enhance this understanding of what underlies our actions and reactions. There was an opportunity for both sides to learn from each other.

During our training, one example shared by the facilitator was that Black people have a tendency to speak with our hands, and to display more emotion when we speak. This is not meant to be a threat, but it is often interpreted that way. This cultural tendency is also often associated with the Latinx community. A White police officer's response, thinking they are at risk, reacts by placing his hand on the handle of his gun. So now my reaction, as a Black civilian who is simply trying to explain his situation is, "Oh so now you want to shoot me?" I flash back to several other encounters I have had as a Black man, weighing less than 140 pounds soaking wet, surrounded by White police officers ready to take me down! And now we are playing an emotional game of chess—action and reaction—which only further escalates the confrontation.

In hindsight, my emotions were high, my logical thinking and intellectual reasoning were low. It made no sense to me. How could a Black executive of a global firm be treated with such indignation? I seriously doubt that any of my White counterparts would have been treated as I was. What also comes to mind is a useful framework I might have used developed by Fons Trompenaars and Charles Hampden-Turner. In their book, *Riding the Waves of Culture*, they introduce seven dimensions that can be used to help understand cultural differences across businesses, industries, and nations. These seven dimensions speak to norms for:

- Relationships and rules (universal versus the particular).
- The group and the individual (individualism vs. communitarianism).
- Feelings and relationships (affective vs. neutral).
- How far we get involved (specific vs. diffuse).
- How we accord status (achievement vs. ascription).
- How we manage time (sequential vs. synchronic).
- How we relate to nature (internal vs. external control).[2]

When thinking of my interactions with the police and with my White coworkers, the dimension from this framework that stands out is "feelings and relationships." In a neutral culture, people tend not to share their emotions. Felt emotions are kept in check and controlled. Individuals come across as cool and rational.

In an affective culture, people tend to share their emotions, even in the workplace. This behavior is accepted and considered normal. Bingo! That was my cultural orientation.

So, the training allowed this perspective to surface and be discussed. It also gave us the opportunity to better understand the motives and biases of the White officers involved. Their norms stemmed from working in an industry culture strongly driven by control and command, rules and regulations, protect and serve. And who exactly were they protecting? Who were they serving? It certainly wasn't me. I wasn't protected. Neither was I served. I was disciplined.

"We protect ourselves, our property, our community, our wives, our daughters." That is their mindset. And for most North Americans, we have been historically conditioned to believe that a threat to this safety is someone or something that is different. This is reinforced by the police department's communication and actions that indicate that Blacks are not welcome in certain communities. It is reiterated on the 5 o'clock news and other media that disproportionately focus on the crimes, poverty, and other negative aspects of the Black community. A Black man driving through a White community triggers a host of unconscious beliefs that a threat is upon us. The police officers were operating from a fixed mindset that I didn't belong there. "He's Black, and up to no good." The numerous documents I presented to substantiate my identity were ignored. The foundational belief that I was a threat overrode any evidence that I might have provided.

As we know, these offensive acts did not start with me and will not end with me, but they continue to be a part of our ecosystem as it relates to police and policing. To borrow from a movie that debuted in 2023, "They [have] cloned Tyronne."

My experience highlights a number of things. One is how bias can manifest in the egregious mistreatment of Black citizens on their way to work. Yet, it also demonstrates that when you have an ally, who is sympathetic and has power, you have an opportunity to take action, elicit a response, and enhance learning within the broader, dominant population. An Ah

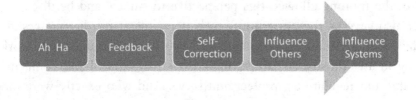

FIGURE 2.1 "Ah Ha" moments framework.

Ha moment manifested for a leader, my CEO, and with additional feedback, he was able to influence others and ultimately influence systemic change (see Figure 2.1)

I'm Being Followed

I've been mad. I've been disappointed, but I've tried to make these experiences a teachable moment. I lean into this because people often don't know what they don't know. I am inspired by my predecessors, like Rosa Parks, who could have gotten up from her seat on the bus in Montgomery, Alabama, but instead decided to lean in and make her defiance a teachable moment.

I've learned to have fun with some of the situations I am in that reflect bias. I relayed this next example in a documentary I was featured in entitled *What About Me*, which discusses the hardships and realities Black men regularly face in America. The documentary takes you through real stories and experiences we have had to endure because of racism in America.

When I worked in Lincolnshire, Illinois, which is about 43 miles outside of Chicago, I would stop and shop in order to avoid traffic rush hours. I remember going to Nieman Marcus quite often. I love Nieman Marcus. I was even trying to convince my wife to name our children Nieman and Marcus, but it just didn't happen.

One day the Nieman's sales rep who got to know me called and said, "We have received some new items; you should come in" and so I did.

I looked at the items, made a purchase, and then began to walk around the store. While looking around, I noticed this guy following me. I knew it was security, so I went back to my sales person, and said, "Listen, somebody's following me. I think he's going to try to rob me. Can you call security?" I played right into the game, knowing exactly what was really going on. She said, "Oh my God, Mr. Stoudemire, let me see what's going on." She then called management and said, "This can't be, we don't have that out here." She found out it was the security guard profiling me and he came and apologized.

I returned every piece of the merchandise I had just purchased and said, "I have been a stellar customer of yours for the last 35 years. I grew up on Nieman Marcus. My mother was a customer, my father was a customer, and this is how you're going to treat me? Take all this merchandise back and cancel my credit card!"

People will forget what you said, people will forget what you did, but people will never forget how you made them feel.

Maya Angelou.

So, this was a teachable moment and an example of how ignoring or minimizing the impacts of bias can be costly for business. Now the impact of my ending my business with this retail chain was relevant but pales in comparison to the 2022 awarding of $4.4 million dollars to a Black man who was racially profiled at a Walmart in Oregon. According to CNN, this customer was not drunk or acting unruly, but was asked to leave when he approached the security guard who was following him.[3] This security guard has since been let go from Walmart, although, reportedly, for reasons unrelated to the complaint.

Defining Bias

Bias is our conscious or subconscious tendency to render judgment automatically about something without thought. In simple terms, bias is a shortcut to interacting with the world around us. Bias is the tipping of the scales, a disproportionate weight in favor of or against a thing, person, or group. Biases can be innate or learned.

With regard to my encounters with the police, I would assert that they had a bias against me because of the melanin in my skin. I was out of place, and it didn't help that I was driving a luxury car.

Do I blame these officers? Well, yes, I do. I believe that they could have taken another approach or simply looked at the evidence more objectively to determine if there was a need to pull me over. Was I speeding? Was there an APB out on me? No! But as humans we regularly take action without pausing to think through what is rational.

Bias can be conscious or unconscious. Unconscious biases, also known as implicit biases, are the underlying attitudes and stereotypes, we may not be aware of, that we attribute to a person or group, and that affect how we engage with that person or group. These are our blind spots, and there is often a disconnect between one's unconscious bias and conscious values. So, looking back at the security guard following me in the store, he might tell you that he values the safety of every individual regardless of their race or gender. But something triggered the bias or stereotype he held that "Blacks are more likely to steal"; and it was his duty to make sure this one (me) didn't get away with it. Unconscious biases are the hardest to change—but it is possible.

Conscious biases are those of which we are aware. If we decide to act on them, we are deliberately choosing to do so ignoring whether or not the decision is based on evidence or fact. Support for a political party, and consequently a political candidate, would be an example where this bias could manifest. Bipartisanship is rooted in bias.

Bias: The Good, the Bad, and the Ugly

Everyone has bias. We are wired for bias. Our brains have components of an Automatic Survival Tendency (AST). What does this mean?

Imagine someone racing toward you with a baseball bat, screaming. That is when your AST had better kick in! It enables you to act instantaneously—to protect yourself. Behaviorally, you will tend to either fight, flee, or freeze. This is the good side of bias and very helpful when there is a *real* threat. The AST is part of the reptilian or oldest part of the brain, the overarching role of which is to minimize threat and maximize reward. This primitive part of the brain is activated as soon as you feel threatened.

Additionally, our AST will deploy in situations whether there exists true danger or not. Something that is different from the norm—like a Black man driving a Mercedes through a White neighborhood—triggers your brain to go into survival mode. The police officers clearly did not flee or freeze. Confronting me in an aggressive way was their AST response. Was their survival threatened? No! But the primitive part of their brains that controls the AST interpreted the situation (me) as threatening.

Our brains are essentially divided into two parts, system one (subconscious) and system two (conscious). Daniel Kahneman published comprehensive research on the neuroscience of bias in his book *Thinking Fast and Slow*.[4] He labeled the two brain systems. System one, the subconscious, was dubbed the fast brain and system two, the conscious, was labeled the slow brain. The fast brain aligns with the AST and can be useful when we are in dangerous situations or need to react quickly, but it also kicks in when we perceive we are in an unknown or new situation. The emotional centers of our brain are aroused.

The slow brain is the one we need to engage to minimize bias. This requires us to pause and reflect before taking action. As many of our mothers schooled us, "Count to 10 before you say or do something you'll regret." This small action can be pivotal in mitigating bias and the more we practice it the more our brains learn to default to this. The key is to recognize when your fast brain is acting and then pause to determine if you have all the information at hand to make the most rational decision.

Our implicit biases also help us when there is an absence of complete information to make quick decisions. So, for example, if we smell smoke nearby, our tendency would most likely be to move out of the area, even in the absence of information that a fire might be burning. If we were to see someone with a strained look on their face who could not communicate with us, our bias might kick in guiding us to check to see if they are in pain or danger. Similarly, a puzzled look on someone's face in a training session would guide a facilitator to ask if there are questions or concerns. All of these examples point to decisions or actions we take without complete information or evidence.

When there is too much information, our bias might be to tune into things that we already believe or to pay attention to the most recent or most repeated messages. Social media has been leveraged to inundate us with gigabytes of new information on what to buy, what to wear, who's hot, and who's not!

Where bias runs amok is when we seek to fill in the blanks, ignore evidence, and take action that is harmful, offensive, or excludes others. These shortcuts affect many of our attitudes and behaviors, such as:

- How we react toward certain people.
- Which aspects of a person we pay most attention to.
- How much we actively listen to what certain people say.
- How much or how little empathy we have for certain people.

Complicating things even more, our underlying and subconscious motivations for how we think and behave are often in conflict with our view of ourselves or rational thought. This is why most individuals would not say they are biased and yet *everybody* is! Even people who are the recipient of bias inevitably perpetuate bias against other groups and sometimes even their own group. Bias is part of the makeup of the world we live in. Biases exist, but this does not mean that we always make decisions or react based on them.

How Individual Bias Manifests in the Workplace

Close to 200 types of bias have been cited on web sources and in the literature. Some of those more commonly associated with the workplace are:

- **Affinity bias** is the tendency to get along with others who are like us. It generally requires less brain effort to engage with individuals who have similar likes, values, beliefs, cultural upbringings, and communication styles. Affinity bias overlaps somewhat with other biases like gender, race, sexual orientation, age, etc. The "good ole boys club" is an example of affinity bias.

- **Appearance bias** is when we associate certain qualities or competencies to a group based on specific physical attributes such as beauty or attractiveness. Beauty bias is a specific type of appearance bias where people believe that attractive people are more successful, competent, and qualified. Research suggests that: "Physically attractive individuals are more likely to be interviewed for jobs and hired, they are more likely to advance rapidly in their careers through frequent promotions, and they earn higher wages than 'so-defined' unattractive individuals." Physical attractiveness is a subjective quality and often reinforced by society and media representations. Consequently, individuals who more closely mirror the dominant members of society may be viewed as being more attractive.

  So, for example, Blacks, Asians, and Hispanics who have a lighter skin tone and European facial features and hair texture are often viewed as more attractive and may benefit more from appearance bias. Having said this, I've noticed a growing trend of Whites trying to acquire phenotypes (physical features) of our sisters and brothers of color via lip injections, butt augmentation, braids and locs . . . and we can't leave out tanning beds. Common manifestations of appearance-based discrimination in hiring also include bias against obese people, tattooed employees, and men with mustaches and beards.

There is also a bias toward height in organizations. Height is correlated with workplace status in organizations. Research conducted by Malcolm Gladwell, as conveyed in his bestselling book *Blink*, indicates that fewer than 15% of American men are over six feet tall, yet almost 60% of corporate CEOs are over six feet.[5]

- **Confirmation bias** refers to the tendency to look for or favor and recall information that confirms beliefs we already hold. This could relate to specific topics or people. For example, if you think that a teammate cannot excel because of their introverted personality, you will find and remember numerous examples of their work activity that supports this and tend to forget anything positive that this teammate has done.

- **Contrast bias** happens when two individuals are judged in comparison to one another, instead of being assessed individually or against a specific standard. This is very common in the selection and performance appraisal processes.

- **Halo and horns biases** occur when a person's impression of one aspect of someone substantially influences their thoughts and feelings about that person as a whole. For example, halo bias would be in effect if a job candidate or employee who has great communication skills is viewed as being effective in all other areas (e.g., analytical skills, strategic planning, inclusive management) where the skill has not been observed. The converse of this would apply to horns bias. Someone with minimum communication skills might be overlooked for roles in financial management where they might in fact be strong.

- **Other culture-based biases** exist. In the United States, there are specific thoughts about how candidates should behave in the interview process that are rooted in culture. For example, *"Candidates should maintain eye contact, dress formally, limit excessive gestures and emotion, self-promote, and smile occasionally during the interview."* This bias may distract us from the true capabilities of an individual as norms for these behaviors can vary by nationality, gender, and age. Additionally, research has found that accents and regional dialects that are different from the dominant group are often distractors in the interview process and correlated with assumptions that the candidate may not be as qualified for the job.

I think of my own regional experience; I grew up in Detroit near the headquarters for Motown. It was the norm to "dress to the nines"! I brought this appreciation for high fashion to Chicago and to the workplace. In comparison to my coworkers, I often found that I was viewed as being overdressed. I believe this biased view of me detracted some from taking me seriously, but also inspired others to spruce it up a bit!

In sum, halo, confirmation, and other types of bias lead us to quick judgments that are more energy-efficient for the brain but are often inaccurate due to our lack of data. We automatically fill in gaps in the information to make a quick decision, but this can often result in wrong conclusions. These bias categories are not mutually exclusive. A number of biases could be operating at the same time.

Bias in Technology

We all have the right to freedom of speech, the right to bear arms, and the right to . . . clean hands, right? Okay, I am being a bit facetious, but here is my point. Bias can seep into the most unsuspecting places, including technology. If a room dominated by White males is designing a product, it will most likely be tested on and usable by White men.

This point came to life on social media in 2015 when it was shown that an automatic soap dispenser was unable to detect a Black customer's hand. As summarized in an article on the website Report, a company called Technical Concepts unintentionally made a discriminatory soap dispenser because the company did not test their product on dark skin tones. The dispenser used near-infrared technology to detect hand motions. Since darker skin tones absorb more light, enough light wasn't reflected back to the sensor to activate the soap dispenser.[6]

There are numerous examples of product/technology design bias. Airport scanners disproportionately set off false alarms based on Black women's textured hair, and turbans and headscarves worn by Muslims and Sikhs. Car crash test dummies are modeled after men in terms of height and weight and may not actually apply standards that are relevant to women or individuals who are smaller in stature. Voice recognition and facial recognition systems disproportionately make errors for Blacks and Asians, leading to more arrests and related mistakes.[7] Complaints, feedback, social media recordings, and, unfortunately, accidents bring these disparities to light. However, this bias is still pervasive.

The automation of processes and products has been taken to a new level with recent developments in artificial intelligence (AI). While there are many benefits that will emanate from the use of AI, for example in treating disease and improving manufacturing, its advances will have disproportionate impacts for Blacks and Hispanics. Blacks and Hispanics are overrepresented in jobs that are at risk for automation and underrepresented in jobs that aren't. A report completed by McKinsey indicates that AI is projected to disrupt 4.5 million jobs for African Americans by 2030.[8] This is a systemic issue that needs to be addressed by our educational, governmental, and private sector institutions; and the time to start doing so is yesterday!

Bias in Systemic Structures

Systemic biases are those maintained by institutions. This could be any institution including educational, judicial/legal, penal, religious, political, healthcare, corporations, industries, media, and the list goes on and on. The biases typically evolve from the values of the privileged or dominant group in these institutions and tend not to favor underrepresented and marginalized groups. I've shared my example of systemic bias in law enforcement and the retail industry. A couple of recent examples of systemic bias at the time of this writing are the Supreme Court's recent dismantling of *Roe v. Wade*—a bias against a woman's right to make decisions about her body and health—and the banning of affirmative action (specifically, race-conscious admissions) in higher education. Historically, when race conscious admissions have been banned in states, admissions of Black and brown students have gone down. This has an indirect but very real impact on corporations. Corporations that pride themselves in recruiting employees from prestigious, predominantly White institutions will find that the pool, and consequently the pipeline, of candidates from diverse backgrounds is diminished.

Another historical example of systemic bias were the Jim Crow laws that were created once slavery was abolished. Separate, but equal was the foundation of this collection of state and local statutes that legalized racial segregation. Named after a Black minstrel show character, these laws were designed to further marginalize Blacks by preventing them from voting, getting an adequate education, or holding meaningful jobs.

Other examples of systemic bias include:

- In healthcare, Black patients are significantly less likely to be prescribed pain medication and generally receive lower doses of it, possibly due to the belief that Whites believe Black people experience less pain.
- In education and corporate sectors, Black students and employees have been penalized or dismissed for wearing braids, locs, and other hairstyles that represent the natural texture of their hair. This has led to the creation of the Crown Act (Creating a Respectful and Open World for Natural Hair).
- Black and brown people are incarcerated at much higher rates than White people. America has approximately 2.3 million people in federal, state, and local prisons and jails, according to a 2020 report

from the nonprofit Prison Policy Initiative.[9] According to a 2018 report from the Sentencing Project, Black men are 5.9 times and Hispanic men are 3.1 times as likely to be incarcerated as White men.[10]

- In a research study conducted by Latino Decisions and the National Hispanic Media Coalition, it was found that negative portrayals of Latinx and immigrants are pervasive in the news and entertainment media.[11] Consequently, individuals who are not Latinx commonly believe many negative stereotypes about these groups are true.

- Attacks on Asian Americans have dramatically increased following the COVID-19 pandemic. As reported in the *Journal of Public Health Management Practices*, "Stereotypes as 'perpetual foreigners' and 'model minorities' reinforce monolithic images of Asians as the 'Other' and a group that does not need help, encouraging structural racism and blocking opportunities."[12]

- A study conducted by the Toronto District School Board (TDSB) has shown that within the educational system, Black students in Toronto experience over-surveillance, which results in a disproportionate number of expulsions.[13]

- In Florida and other states, the history of European Americans is viewed as acceptable American History to teach in schools, while the history of other cultural groups has been eradicated from the curricula.

- Research findings indicate that teachers assume that students from Asian American cultures will excel in math and that girls will not excel in the STEM areas. Such biases often become self-fulfilling prophecies.

- In the corporate sector, the use of certain performance evaluation systems exacerbates bias. Horns/halo bias has often been viewed as one that can seep into the performance appraisal process. Recent literature associates this bias with the 9-box grid used to evaluate employees. Employees are placed in a box within a 3-by-3 matrix and labeled based on their performance and potential. A 2022 research study analyzing 9-box data for almost 30,000 employees found that women receive substantially lower "potential" ratings than men, despite receiving higher job performance ratings.[14] During the course of my career I have observed this process and while I recognize the merits of it for identifying high-potential talent, all too often I have observed leaders using subjective criteria to rate individuals. It is also not a transparent process, as often those being evaluated do not receive any feedback on where they stand, and unknowingly go through their workdays being unfavorably labeled. All they see is their unsuccessful attempts to move up the ladder. This disappointment can lead to disengagement, a fixed mindset, and quiet quitting.

These examples demonstrate that just because something exists as a policy or law does not make it right. There were laws that upheld slavery, that upheld lynching. Systemic bias, racism, and sexism are often protected and perpetuated by those in power. Consequently, galvanizing the support of powerful allies is a step toward change. This is not an easy task, but it is a necessary part of the strategy to create empathy, action, equity, and care.

While resolving systemic bias may seem like a lofty goal, we can make inroads by addressing our individual biases. Change starts with you!

Tactical Tools/Considerations

Our biases don't always have negative implications; and because we have biases, doesn't mean we will always act on them. We may not be able to eliminate our biases, but we can manage them.
Individuals can:

- Acknowledge that you have bias. It is human nature and not always negative.

- Leverage self-assessment tools. One widely researched tool is The Implicate Association Test (IAT). The IAT measures attitudes and beliefs that you may not be aware of and helps you understand specific categories in which bias may be occurring. The IAT measures the strength of associations you make between concepts (e.g., Black people, women) and evaluations (e.g., good, bad) or stereotypes (e.g., good dancers, nurturing, etc.).
- Engage in reframing. Let's say you recognize that you associate Black men with aggression and being out of control. If you catch yourself thinking this, a reframe would be: "Black men are energetic, passionate about what they believe in, and spontaneous."
- Employ dialogue and perspective taking. This would involve gathering insights from others, especially those who think differently than you. We learn from difference!
- Practice immersion. Shadowing someone for a week to better understand their world and lived experience helps build empathy and enables you to reflect on any assumptions you may have. Travel, in which you engage with and learn from local residents helps to break down biases, as well.

Organizational leaders and practitioners can:

- Solicit feedback. Reach out to employees to gauge their perspectives on where they feel bias is showing up within the workplace. This enables you to test your assumptions and take appropriate action. Remember that the employee experience includes the things that happen on their commute back and forth to work, as well.
- Identify teachable moments. Establish and facilitate formal and informal forums for employees to engage in storytelling

about personal experiences to advance awareness and empathy (e.g., cross-cultural mentoring, Candid Conversation sessions, Lunch and Learns, etc.).

- Offer implicit bias training. Require leadership to partake in this initially and then cascade throughout the organization.
- Create a repository of resources on bias. Set up a portal that has links to articles, podcasts, advocacy organizations, and other resources to help employees continue their learning and skill development as it relates to addressing bias.
- Identify opportunities to debunk negative stereotypes and biases. Invite speakers from diverse backgrounds with expertise in areas not typically associated with their cultural identity, e.g., women working in aeronautics, Latina CEOs.

3

Will vs. Skill

Putting Skill into Perspective

There are multiple overlapping pieces in this puzzling phenomenon I refer to as "Will vs. Skill." In this chapter, I will explore several scenarios in which this dichotomy is demonstrated. Each scenario speaks to the misconceptions, challenges, and pathways to advancing DEI within organizations by looking closely at the role of an individual's skill alongside other motivating factors.

To begin, I will share my observations on the individuals who are leading DEI functions. Many have the will but not the skill. Additionally, the capacity to have impact within the organization is often limited by the absence of resources and sponsorship.

A second scenario is one where individuals with strong technical skills are promoted into people management and leadership roles. They have specific skills that do not necessarily translate into their newly acquired positions, and which can deter efforts to create an inclusive work environment.

A third phenomenon I've noticed is the rigidity or bias inherent in the criteria used to evaluate someone's skill level and their potential to advance, particularly for people of color. I have experienced and observed that the openness to look at alternative indicators of prior success are limited to what falls within the scope of "organizational norms."

Next, I will explore Intent vs. Impact at both the individual and organizational levels. There is often a will to do the right thing, but blind spots often prevent us from understanding how our actions are perceived by others.

I will close out this chapter with a discussion of the value of partnerships. I have found that joining forces with internal and external groups, that can provide skilled resources and perspective through another lens, is ultimately good for an organization's triple bottom line (people, profits, planet).

Leading DEI: Will and Skill

When I think of how will vs. skill shows up, I can reflect on some of the people in companies in which I have provided consulting to wanting to do the work of DEI. They care about it; they might even say they are passionate about it. But they really don't know what to do. They don't know how to enter difficult and uncomfortable conversations. They don't want to be offensive or say the wrong thing. Basically, they're afraid of taking a risk. They really want to do well, but they're not equipped. They're not able to lead effectively, influence or have conversations in this area without some additional learning and reinforcement. They often need coaches and allies to support them.

In many organizations, you will find DEI practitioners in roles that support other senior leaders but are not considered senior leader roles. It has evolved over the years. The role of Chief Diversity Officer or Global DEI officer is relatively new compared to other executive-level positions.

When we look at the evolution of the diversity practitioner role, we can start with looking at how diversity, equity, and inclusion as a practice has advanced within organizations. Figure 3.1 maps out this progression.

Organizations began looking at DEI from a compliance perspective. They were required to complete EEO-1 reports to verify what their

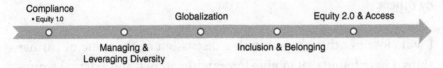

FIGURE 3.1 Evolution of the DEI practitioner role.

workforce composition looked like and how closely it matched the availability of various demographic groups in the labor force. So, where there was underutilization of a specific group, proactive or affirmative actions were required to be put in place. Organizations that needed to comply were those that were governmental or received funds from the government. The focus was primarily on representation. How many Xs do we have in our organization? How many Ys have been promoted in the past year? Is the rate that Zs are leaving our organization proportionate to overall workforce attrition? This practice I will refer to as Equity 1.0.

The compliance mindset evolved into "OK, now how do we effectively manage all of these Xs, Ys, and Zs?" This is when we saw diversity and sensitivity training pop up everywhere. Around the same time, you heard practitioners speak to how to leverage diversity. This was an attempt to benefit from the unique insights and lived experience of certain individuals, particularly as it helped the organization address marketplace needs.

As companies expanded their footprint by entering new markets and outsourcing, diversity took on a global focus. The next phase of diversity work focused on creating inclusive work environments and a sense of belonging. More recently, Equity 2.0 has resurfaced as well as a focus on Access. We are looking at equity in a more holistic and systemic manner. Advocacy for social justice movements has been evident across each of the phases and has been given a lot of attention recently due to the high visibility of polarized groups and movements, captured real time via social media.

During the summer of 2020, the United States saw a surge in promotions of individuals into Chief Diversity Officer roles. Recommitment statements were pervasive on company websites and other social media espousing a company's dedication to DEI. This was following the murder of George Floyd. Was it corporate guilt? Was it a collective rage that brought about the need to respond? I'm sure that both of these reasons applied, depending on the company. I also know that two years later, I've noticed many corporations now questioning their commitment to DEI, given the 2023 Supreme Court ruling prohibiting the use of affirmative action in higher education.

Now, let's take a look at who we see in these DEI practitioner roles and how they are resourced. There are certain DEI practitioners who solely focus on workforce issues, strategies, and organizational culture. Others look at diversity, equity, inclusion, and access within their company's supply chain, as well. Still others combine this work with strategies to better understand the needs of multicultural markets and communities that are consumers to their organizations. The Global DEI officer has the added responsibility of discerning and harmonizing processes across borders. See Figure 3.2.

Those who are in this role are usually a department of one and have to leverage through others. If they do have a professional reporting to them, it is usually in a matrix fashion.

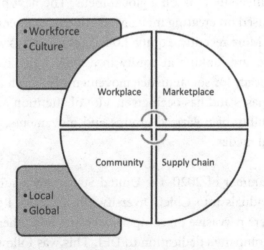

FIGURE 3.2 DEI practitioner focus areas.

The backgrounds that practitioners come from is wide-ranging. Some started off in Human Resources (HR) or another talent management area. Others have come from Corporate Social Responsibility functions or related community-facing roles. Yet, a good number have come from different business sectors that have nothing to do with diversity, equity, and inclusion or the need to challenge aspects of the organization's culture. I'm not saying that it's all bad, but it speaks to the learning curve for those who are entering the space; and, historically, moving into this role has been one where the incumbent is not receiving, but creating their own on-the-job training.

Because of the varying backgrounds from which diversity practitioners were emerging and a desire to set standards for this role, organizations and institutions, such as the Society for Human Resources (SHRM), Cornell University, and others began building training certifications for DEI. University curriculums are also now offering degree specializations in DEI.

CDOs and other DEI practitioners are often performing this function alongside another full-time role. And no, the salary does not reflect two full-time roles! In what other strategic function does this happen? I've heard from some of my colleagues in academia that as full-time faculty they were asked to take on the DEI officer responsibilities for their institutions. In the corporate sector, those who have a full-time role in public relations and marketing were asked to add DEI to the mix. Fortunately, I have been able to avoid this dilemma. Yet, how can you expect anyone to be effective or have impact under such conditions? There are often competing demands in which deliverables from the core role take priority. Yet the incumbent is still accountable for DEI outcomes and the obvious scapegoat if anything goes awry.

This insight is backed up by a 2019 survey conducted by Russell Reynolds Associates. In a survey of 97 CDOs working in the business sector, the data suggested that CDOs were not "well-equipped to spearhead necessary organizational changes" due to three major pain points. First, CDOs have many responsibilities, with 53% holding an additional role unrelated to diversity and inclusion. More than half of CDOs were not resourced appropriately with staff or had the necessary skills, impacting their ability to maximize results. Second, CDOs seemed to be missing or underutilizing essential diversity and inclusion data. Only 35% of CDOs had employee demographic data, 69% tracked employee survey results, and only 28% believed that formal employee surveys drive diversity strategies. Perhaps these findings resulted because of a lack of analytics, expertise, or resources to support the work. Lastly, diversity was disconnected from the business strategy, with only 27% of CDOs saying the business strategy is a driver of diversity and inclusion strategies.[1]

DEI practitioners are constantly challenging the status quo so this individual has to leverage change management skills, influence skills, and diagnostic and assessment skills to do so. What is concerning is that the practitioner will typically work with an organization that does not feel the need to address its organizational culture and looks at the practitioner as some kind of a miracle worker—someone who can attract and retain individuals from visibly or apparently diverse backgrounds, but who fit in with the culture and who *don't rock the boat*! Square pegs! Round holes!

I present these observations not to paint a picture of overwhelm, but to emphasize that the DEI practitioner role is one that you cannot do in your sleep. It requires a range of skills, competencies, and a certain temperament. One has to balance being an advocate with being realistic about when to push and match the culture. One has to use judgment around where incremental progress is sufficient and what areas require transformational change. It can be a thankless job; and someone has to have the will or passion. It takes someone who loves the kind of work that they're doing, and feels a sense of personal gratification, as often the recognition and support from others is not there. And we can't leave out energy, a thick skin, and the ability to detach from your work while staying connected to what is happening outside of work. I could go on and on here.

This high-level overview is meant to emphasize the growing complexity of the DEI practitioner role and to affirm that both will and a comprehensive body of knowledge, skill, and competency are needed to lead and influence in this arena.

Technical Skill and Inclusive Leadership: Mixing Apples and Oranges

When I think of how leaders are often identified, what comes to mind is the Peter Principle—that you are promoted to your level of incompetence. I have witnessed numerous individuals being promoted in an organization into leadership roles because of their track record in completing various project work, or who contribute in a way that brings results. But the rub is, they're not very good at managing other people. And the irony is that many of these individuals will tell you that they don't even want to manage people; they just want to be in a leadership role. According to their organizations, they have all of the college degrees and pedigrees to do the functional work, and so it is assumed they would also be good leaders in their functional areas. That is halo bias operating. These individuals' ability to effectively communicate, galvanize, influence others, develop others, etc., is totally overlooked. This is problematic, in general, as it often results in lowered morale, engagement, and productivity on their teams. This becomes even more notable when it comes to leading diverse teams and creating an inclusive work environment.

Let's say that someone does have people management experience. It can't be assumed that they will also demonstrate inclusive leadership. Numerous leaders have a directive and prescriptive leadership style—command and control, do it my way or no way at all. This clearly minimizes any efforts to advance DEI. And once they're given feedback on this, they may still have the will to do the work, but they still don't have the skills or temperament, namely the skill of active listening.

Additionally, in many organizations in the private sector, there is an over emphasis on results. Organizations are often mesmerized by someone who can deliver results . . . regardless of the process followed or the participation of relevant stakeholders, such as those impacted by the outcomes. A disproportionate focus on delivering results without looking at the systemic and human impacts often contradicts efforts to create cultures of inclusion.

So, what is involved in inclusive leadership? There are a number of components including general interpersonal skills like communication, active listening, and influence. Some of the most important aspects of inclusive leadership are shown in Figure 3.3. It involves emotional intelligence, general intelligence, and cross-cultural intelligence or competency. It involves modeling the behaviors you want to see in others. Most importantly, it requires commitment to continuous learning.

General intelligence is a prerequisite for being able to function in most areas. The components that I believe are most relevant to inclusive leadership include critical thinking (or the ability to analyze and evaluate an issue from many different angles), which helps with problem solving and solution generation.

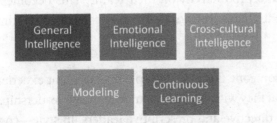

FIGURE 3.3 Requisite skills and behaviors for inclusive leadership.

Borrowing from the many frameworks on *emotional intelligence*, the key aspects that have relevance to inclusive leadership include self-awareness, awareness of the impact one has on others, empathy, and relationship management.

Cross-cultural intelligence or competency is the awareness of one's own cultural filters and ability to discern and take into consideration other worldviews. Culturally competent leaders should be able to recognize that their definition of leadership is most likely aligned with their cultural upbringing and values. Cross-cultural competence also involves the demonstrated skill of interacting effectively with individuals from different cultural backgrounds; and the ability to adopt an ethnorelative/multicultural approach when seeking solutions.

Because this is such an important skill to build in leadership and across the organization, I want to take a deeper dive into this competency.

The reference to cross-cultural competency is pervasive in corporations, social service agencies, healthcare, and the media. Other related terms include intercultural competency and cross-cultural humility (which proposes that you never master cross-cultural interactions, and always have something to learn).

Cross-cultural competency has been associated with a number of constructs. It is not fixed and so can be developed over time. Some of my takeaways from the various models that exist are that cross-cultural intelligence begins with self-awareness. These are the insights gained through the Ah Ha moments that I talked about in Chapter 1. They can be gained through feedback from individuals or an assessment someone has taken. Self-awareness helps one uncover their blind spots, understand their biases, and better understand the cultural filters that they are applying in different situations.

Cross-cultural competency is also based on knowledge about different demographic groups. This obviously takes time, exposure, immersion, conversation, and action. But one has to be careful here. As the saying goes, a little bit of knowledge can be a dangerous thing. I've often seen employees attend one training session on bias or organizational culture, walking out and feeling a brand new level of bravery to explore and put in the application what they learned. Under the guise of curiosity, they may ask personal questions about someone's hair texture or heritage. This often leads to stereotyping or offending others. Knowledge is something that needs to be checked and rechecked. A little bit of knowledge can lead to a lot of assumptions.

A construct that has been associated with cross-cultural competency is personality. There are certain personality factors that lend themselves toward developing this competency. Referencing the five-factor personality model OCEAN[2]—Openness (to experience), Conscientiousness, Extraversion, Agreeableness, and Neuroticism (emotional instability)—Openness is the one that is most often associated with cross-cultural competency. Someone who is open-minded demonstrates curiosity about things that are different. Someone with an open mind will most likely also challenge their own assumptions and allow vulnerability to surface. They are more likely to actively listen to others versus just listening to respond, and they are more likely to engage in self-reflection.

Experience and exposure are also linked to cross-cultural competence. The more one has interacted with different democratic groups facilitates them being able to recognize different worldviews and differentiate them from their own worldview. It doesn't necessarily mean that someone is going to demonstrate the skill, as they may feel uncomfortable or feel that one worldview or way of doing things is superior to another. This polarization is evident in the Developmental Model of Intercultural Sensitivity—DMIS.[3, 4]

This DMIS (see Figure 3.4) represents various orientations that reflect how we respond to cultural differences. The Intercultural Development Inventory was developed to measure where one falls on this continuum.[5]

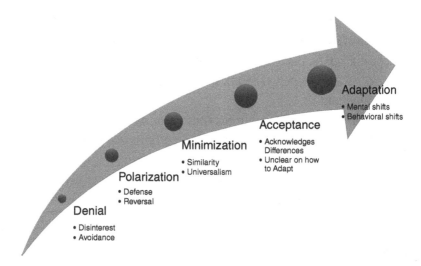

FIGURE 3.4 The developmental model of intercultural sensitivity.

It is an excellent tool for creating common language within an organization and coaching leaders and employees on how they can improve upon their capabilities to navigate cultural differences.

The Intercultural Development Inventory

- ***Denial:*** *An orientation that recognizes more observable cultural differences (e.g., food), but may not notice deeper cultural difference (e.g., conflict resolution styles) and may avoid or withdraw from such differences.*
- ***Polarization:*** *A judgmental orientation that views cultural difference in terms of "us" and "them" This ranges from (1) a more uncritical view toward one's own cultural values and practices coupled with an overly critical view toward other cultural values and practices (Defense) to (2) an overly critical orientation toward one's own cultural values and practices and an uncritical view toward other cultural values and practices (Reversal).*

- *Minimization:* An orientation that highlights cultural commonality and universal values and principles that may also mask deeper recognition and appreciation of cultural differences.
- *Acceptance:* An orientation that recognizes and appreciates patterns of cultural difference and commonality in one's own and other cultures.
- *Adaptation:* An orientation that can shift cultural perspective and change behavior in culturally appropriate and authentic ways.

Mitchell Hammer, 2006, 2007

Another one of my favorite models to reference and use in helping organizations understand and navigate cultural differences is the Seven Dimensions of Culture framework. I spoke to this in Chapter 2, Say It Isn't So: How Bias Overrides Evidence, as I was reflecting on my encounters with law enforcement. To briefly recap, in their book, *Riding the Waves of Culture*, Fons Trompenaars and Charles Hampden-Turner introduce seven dimensions that can be used to help understand cultural differences across businesses, industries, and nations.[6]

The Seven Dimensions of Culture

- *Relationships and Rules (Universal vs. the Particular)* – Universalism basically asserts that what is good and right always applies, while particularism puts more weight on the unique situation and obligation to relationships.
- *The Group and the Individual (Individualism vs. Communitarianism)* – The contrast between these two dimensions is

anchored in whether we put ourselves as a person first in a group, or whether we put the importance of the group first.

- ***Feelings and Relationships (Affective vs. Neutral)*** *– This juxtaposition looks at the extent to which we feel expressing emotions is acceptable or whether our interactions should be objective and detached.*

- ***How Far we Get Involved (Specific vs. Diffuse)*** *– The Specific orientation suggests that you limit your interactions with others to particular contexts (e.g., at work only). The Diffuse cultural orientation would be one in which you feel it is preferable to engage with individuals in many aspects of your life, both professional and personal.*

- ***How we Accord Status (Achievement vs. Ascription)*** *– We judge individuals on their record of accomplishments and achievements and on things that are attributable to aspects like birth, kinship and other relationships, gender, age, and credentials.*

- ***How we Manage Time (Sequential vs. Synchronic)*** *– In sequential cultures, the emphasis is on completing tasks in discrete elements, one by one, with a clear start and finish. In synchronic cultures, past and present are fused together and there is more tolerance to interruptions of the sequence. For example, someone with a synchronic orientation might feel very comfortable interrupting a business meeting to take a call from a relative who just arrived in town.*

- ***How we Relate to Nature (Internal vs. External Control)*** *– Specific cultures view the major impacts on their life as being within their internal control; while other cultures view nature or external events in the world as being more powerful and something to be revered or feared.*

Fons Trompenaars and Charles Hampden-Turner (1998).

I have used both of the frameworks presented extensively in my work as a DEI practitioner. In subsequent chapters, I will comment on some of the Ah Ha moments I have witnessed leaders experience as they discuss and debrief on these frameworks. Building cross-cultural competency is pivotal. Demonstrating it, through modeling, is transformational.

Modeling requires that a leader first know what behaviors, visible to others, can facilitate an inclusive environment. Behaviors such as seeking multiple perspectives, demonstrating curiosity, showing comfort with being vulnerable, and a willingness to admit mistakes and move forward from lessons learned. I have seen one leader's invitation for others to challenge her point of view in a staff meeting create a new and inspiring dynamic for inclusive and candid conversations.

Continuous learning is a must. Recognizing that building awareness and skill is not a "one and done," leaders and all employees must commit to learning, unlearning, and relearning on a continual basis. Attending a couple of sessions on implicit bias and microinequities does not a guru make! In my experience, being curious, open-minded to other points of view, and willing to take the time to explore and discuss uncomfortable cultural issues, in both individual and group forums, is a critical pathway to inclusive leadership and inclusive organizations.

Similar to building excellent presentation skills, financial skills, or negotiation skills, there are many frameworks and principles we can reference, but we still have to put in the work. And we must realize that what we applied in one situation can't always be precisely replicated in another with the same outcome. For example, the negotiation tactics you use to mediate a tense relationship between union representatives and management are somewhat relevant but not fully applicable to the negotiation tactics you would use in a hostage situation. Context matters!

Success of inclusive leadership is dependent on individual skills and an individual's will, but it is also connected to the extent to which the collective organization's systems, practices, policies, and norms promote an inclusive work environment.

Minimizing Alternate Pathways

As far back as I can remember, the importance of getting a good education was emphasized within my family, church, and other social groups. It was supposed to be the great equalizer; or at least give Black Americans a chance to compete on the corporate playing field. I started out on the pathway to get a higher education; but I didn't finish my degree. My mother died my second year in college. This had rippling emotional and financial impacts on my family. I had to help out my sister and her two-year-old. I was knocked into several circumstances where I had to fend for myself, and that did not make college a feasible option.

So, I have learned to do things differently, to prove my capabilities. I've had to work twice as hard to get ahead. Heck, I've had to work harder to even be considered or acknowledged. My definition of working hard, though, was not confined to the task at hand. I became very adept at making connections and building relationships that led to outputs, outcomes, and impact. As an example, I have built up an expansive network within my community. I took on leadership roles within my church when none were available within my company. I became indispensable in helping to strategize, plan events, manage projects and people in this setting. The relationships that I built within the community I was able to extend into the workplace. For example, I was able to connect one of the Employee Network Groups from a former employer with then Senator Barack Obama in an up close and personal discussion on diversity in organizations.

I was also able to leverage my connection with John W. Rogers, Jr. and Mellody Hobson, co-CEOs of Ariel Investments. When our company went public, Ariel had bought shares and John indicated that he wanted to meet with our CEO. The CEO and I had developed a close working relationship and were discussing how we could reach specific goals. One was to increase diverse representation in our higher pay bands. Another was to increase the diversity of our shareholders. I mentioned to the CEO that my good friend John wanted to meet with him. He didn't get excited about the idea. In fact, he kind of brushed it off.

I continued to press the issue and he said, "I will make sure to say hello to him at the next stockholder's meeting." My response was, "Humor me, if you will. Verify the amount of stock that John owns and let that determine whether you have a one-on-one with him. I think it's fairly significant." He looked at me like "yeah, yeah, yeah," and the meeting was pretty much over.

I headed back to my office but before I could sit down, I got a call from the CEO's assistant saying that he wanted me to come back immediately! So, I went back to his office. Our CEO was in awe as, upon investigation, he had discovered that John's firm, Ariel Investments, was the second largest shareholder of our company. He apologized and realized that this was an Ah Ha moment for him. He had made assumptions but at least, he was curious enough to check out the data.

My CEO was very open to meeting with John after that. In John's true style, he agreed to the meeting only if I could attend. John was very much into sponsoring individuals who he mentored and taking them to meetings with him. In fact, his current co-CEO, Mellody Hobson, started at Ariel as an intern. She shadowed and accompanied John to his various meetings and eventually advanced into her executive role.

Ariel's meeting with our CEO ultimately led to a collaborative partnership producing groundbreaking research. The study looked at the different practices of Blacks versus Whites relative to how retirement funds were utilized. This collaborative research was replicated in 60 large U.S.

organizations representing 2.4 million employees and made national news. Ah Ha! Money talks!

Over the years, my managers have seen the value I bring but I have often received initial recognition from individuals and groups outside of my organization. For example, The 100 Black Men Chicago chapter hosted a reception for me celebrating a new executive role I had obtained. It was their way of acknowledging my success as well as showing gratitude for my long-standing commitment and dedication to the organization. More than 800 people showed up for the event. It included notables such as the former governor of Illinois Pat Quinn; Mayor Rahm Emanuel; the former president of McDonald's, Don Thompson; the CEO of BMO Harris Bank, Mark Furlong; the CEO of Northern Trust bank, Rick Waddell; and John Rogers and Mellody Hobson, co-CEOs of Ariel Investments. In addition, there was a personalized video from First Lady Michelle Obama and President Barack Obama. More than 300 members from my church attended as well. They were walking up and down the halls of the hotel singing gospel songs while rubbing the walls of the building with holy anointing oil to ensure my success!

My chairman of the board got wind of the celebration and called me. He asked, "What is this shindig that all of my peers got invited to that I wasn't invited to?" Given that I did not control the invite list, I said, "Certainly, you are more than welcome to come. If you do come, I would love for you to make some remarks." He replied, "I am scheduled to fly out in my private jet to meet my wife in London that day, but I will reschedule my flight." Because he decided to come, he then encouraged all other senior executives to attend as well.

It was a lavish event! People were overtaken by the beauty of the grand hotel, the food, the extravagant décor, the many posters of me on the wall. The ambiance was breathtaking! Everyone in attendance was so excited for me. This was the first time my employer had brought a Black man into the DEI role at the senior vice president level. It was a watershed move on their part that demonstrated their commitment to prioritizing diversity, equity, and inclusion.

When it came time for remarks, Dr. Byron Brazier, pastor of the Apostolic Church of God, said to the crowd, "Tyronne is a creative type. He's not going to do things the way that you might do things. But don't worry, and just stay out of his way, because at the end of the day, he is going to make us all look good!"

My chairman's comments were short, but they made the point. He extended a warm welcome to me to the leadership team. "Welcome to the family." Looking out into the vast crowd of supporters that had amassed for this evening of luxurious celebration, he then added, "I am no fool. I work for Tyronne!" The crowd roared!

I knew I had the will, I did things to gain the skill, and ultimately this gave me credibility in the workplace. But the journey to reaching this level was a long one and not without its hurdles. Early in my career, I was not seriously considered for opportunities because of my race and gender, where I grew up, the schools I attended, and degrees I had or did not have on my resume.

I remember an interview I had regarding a global management position. The hiring manager said, "Well, you don't have a global background." I assume he meant that I hadn't been an expatriate in another country, but that was a limited definition. I told him, "If you read my resume, you will see that I helped set up call centers in Dubai, New Delhi, and Germany, and I have facilitated training in all those areas." He overlooked this and jumped to the conclusion that I didn't have a global background. The job relevant experience and transferrable leadership skills I had developed and demonstrated outside of work were also discounted.

This experience epitomizes the work presented in a 2005 *Harvard Business Review* article, "Leadership in Your Midst: Tapping the Hidden

Strengths of Minority Executives." Written by Sylvia Ann Hewlett, Carolyn Buck Luce, and Cornel West, this article speaks to the variety of ways that Blacks have developed and demonstrated leadership skills within their churches or their communities. These skills and competencies are transferable to corporate America but are overlooked.[7] For example, being a president of a traveling choir of 350 people responsible for the wardrobe, transportation, and all logistics in between speaks directly to project management, execution skills, and problem solving. Experiences, such as playing a leadership role in a sorority, fraternity, or for a global organization like the "Jack and Jills" or Links, is often not shared by job candidates, either, as they assume it will not be viewed as relevant or align with the organizational culture.

My nontraditional profile led recruiters and hiring managers to believe I wasn't prepared for certain roles. This is the lived experience for many candidates of color. However, this is not the story for White men in our country.

In fact, the literature shows that a White man will be given an opportunity and will take it even if he's not prepared. He is able to do so because he has built up his social capital (internal relationships and networks, sponsorship, etc.). Women and people of color often take a risk averse approach in pursing opportunities, and say, "Well, I need another degree. I want to get a specific certification. It's not a good time right now because I want to get my kids off to college." The focus is more on human capital (education and training) as a pathway to advancement.

But even with all the credentials and degrees one might pursue, it is often still not enough. I recall bringing a new hire at an individual contributor level into one of my employer's change management areas. This individual came in with a PhD. When her name came up in our key talent discussions, I would hear comments like, "I like Debra [not her real name]. She's a lovely person, nice, smart, and approachable but I don't think she would make a good leader or should move into the next pay band." I thought, "Wow, have you even looked at her resume? Have you checked out her credentials? If bringing a PhD and decades of experience, including VP of a practice area at a niche consulting firm, doesn't warrant you taking a second look, then I'm missing something here." Debra's career trajectory was on somewhat of a roller coaster but at some point she had a manager who knew of her strengths from a former organization and who decided to visibly sponsor her. Debra was moved into a more strategic role where her contribution was more widely noted and her pay band increased. Sponsorship matters!

An additional insight I have that is related to the discounting of skills and experiences of people of color, particularly Blacks and Latinx employees, relates to communication skills. I have found the evaluation of communication skills to be highly subjective and biased. As I mentioned in the previous chapter, my style of expression was generally more expressive and animated than my White colleagues. I also happened to be working for a very conservative, nonconfrontative organization. I remember that as we were auditing the performance review outcomes, we discovered that every Black person who was in leadership had the same development opportunity around communications. "James doesn't effectively communicate. His writing and oral communication skills need development . . ." This was a cut and paste in everybody's performance review, but it wasn't a performance issue, it was a cultural difference. Being more emotional or expressive did not mesh with the more neutral, conservative tone of the majority. Additionally, I suspect that the direct and candid approach used by Black and Latinx employees brought discomfort to our White managers and teammates. In Kochman's classic work *Black and White Styles in Conflict*, he addresses these differences.

> When Blacks and Whites engage each other in public debate about an issue, they are divided not only over content—the issue itself— but, more fundamentally, over process: how disagreement on an issue is to be appropriately handled . . . The Black mode—that of

Black community [inner city] people—is high-keyed: animated, interpersonal, and confrontational. The White mode—that of the middle class—is relatively low-keyed: dispassionate, impersonal, and non-challenging.

Kochman's work from 1983 may not capture all that we know about cultural differences today, but it is still relevant to explaining how norms developed around majority cultures have the tendency to minimize behaviors that fall outside of the norm.

I hope that a key takeaway from this section is that there are many pathways to success. Skill and competency can be measured in multiple ways. They need not be transfixed by tradition or dominant cultural norms. We can avoid this bias and making mistakes that exclude marginalized groups by having more conversations that explore alternative pathways.

Speaking of mistakes . . .

Intent vs. Impact: Microinequities and Pigeonholing Are Birds of the Same Feather

Have you ever made a seemingly innocent remark to someone or some group and unexpectedly met with a response of dismay, disbelief, or disgust? If you are human, most likely you have. Good intentions are not enough.

So how does one discern when one's intent may be disconnected from the impact. Perhaps you were being curious when you reached out to touch your coworker's locs. You may have thought someone wanted you speaking on their behalf in the meeting when their point was ignored. And what is the big fuss about what you did anyway? Aren't we being too sensitive these days? Separating the wheat from the chaff, or the intent from the impact, takes time and, to beat a dead cliché to death, intention! It involves honing self-awareness, awareness of the impact you have on others, awareness of the group dynamics in the room, and *skill*. To be competent in any arena requires unlearning, learning, practice, and learning some more. Understanding offenses has been addressed in much of the literature on microinequities.

First proposed in 1970 by Dr. Chester Pierce,[9] and resurrected by Columbia University professor Derald Wing Sue,[10] *microinequities are the everyday verbal, nonverbal, and environmental slights, snubs, or insults, whether intentional or unintentional, that communicate hostile, derogatory, or negative messages to target persons based solely upon their marginalized group membership.* They are:

- Verbal, behavioral, or environmental slights.
- Often automatic and unintentional.
- Occur in brief instances on a daily basis.
- Communicate hostile, derogatory, or negative viewpoints.
- Perpetuate exclusion.

Microinequities seem to be innocuous mistakes but they have damaging impacts. They erode and chip away one's self esteem. In a book by Harvard professor Alvin Poussaint (*Death by a Thousand Nicks*), he speaks to the cumulative impact of microinequities. He proposes that dealing with microaggressions or microinequities on a weekly basis has both health related and behavioral ramifications for the workplace.[11]

Those who truly want to be a part of culture change would benefit by recognizing how microinequities play out taking stock of their own behavior to minimize them, and knowing what to do and what not to do. They often play out as assaults, insults, or remarks that invalidate a person's identity. Micro assaults are generally intentional offenses and are less common in most industries. Micro invalidations and micro insults are often unintentional and more commonly practiced.

These are some examples:

- Assault: Telling a joke that mocks or degrades a racial/ethnic group, someone who is differently abled or someone's gender identity. "How many blind people does it take to screw in a light bulb?"
- Insult: Feeling the need to explain the comments made by a person of color or woman as if they aren't able to do so on their own. "I think what Pat is trying to say is . . ."
- Invalidation: Discounting someone's identity. "I don't see color when I think of you. You're just like everyone else here."

While microinequities are generally discussed from the perspective of race and racism, any marginalized group in our society may become targets: people of color, women, LGBTQ+ individuals, those who are differently abled, religious minorities, etc.

The dilemma is that those perpetrating these offenses are often, although not always, unaware that they are doing so. The person on the receiving end will typically not acknowledge that they have been offended. They may question whether or not they heard correctly, what did she mean by that, am I being too sensitive, or more apathetically, no one will support me if I say something, it will just make things worse.

According to a survey done by Unstoppable Performance Leaders (UPL), 93% of women think reporting noninclusive behaviors, like microinequities and harassment, will negatively impact their careers.[12]

Additionally, if one's company culture does not encourage or model confrontation or open and honest conversations, this can further diminish individuals speaking up for themselves or for someone else.

I don't want to be known as the "Angry Black Woman"!

Training in this area is a step in the right direction as it helps raise awareness around the types of behavior that lead to microinequities.

Training gives individuals a chance to discuss and share their experiences with microinequities. And it gives participants language and ways to address microinequities.

For inclusive leaders who witness a microinequity, they could use it as a teachable moment. For example, if you hear a White male colleague repeating the same idea that a Black female colleague just presented, you could stop and say, "I like that idea, I noticed that Val made that point a few minutes ago. Val, would you agree? This freezes the frame and enables everyone to reflect on the group dynamic that just occurred, gives Val a chance to agree or not, given you may assume she meant the same thing, and minimizes the need to chastise Bill, given he may have truly thought that the idea he shared was an original one.

There might also be times where you as a leader say or do something that you later learn was offensive. Learn from this as well. If you have the opportunity, apologize for the impact your behavior had; indicate what your objective was; and ask for feedback on what you might have done differently. Be ready for candor, if you decide to take this approach!

I regularly am on the receiving in of both micro- and macroinequities—unintended and intended. I've gotten to the point where I feel very comfortable advocating for myself and using the opportunity as a teachable moment. However, I realize that not all of my brothers and sisters feel this way. My insight for you is to:

- Take a breath before reacting. Remember the wisdom of counting to 10.
- Approach the offender, giving the benefit of the doubt. "I assume you thought you were complimenting me, but . . ."
- Focus on the behavior, not the person. "I assume you thought you were complimenting me, when you said, 'Wow, you completed this report all by yourself?' however, I felt you were questioning my capability and honesty . . ."

Microinequities illustrate how one's intent differs from the impact it has on others. Intent vs. impact applies to both individual behaviors as well as systemic practices and policies. Pigeonholing is one example. The intent in this organizational practice may have been to leverage diversity but taken to the extreme it often exploits individuals or prevents employees in general from reaching their full potential (the impact). Leaders will indicate that they value employees for their unique perspectives, for example a woman's perspective on creating a new product for customers who are women. These female employees get tapped into for similar projects. The rub (impact) is that they don't necessarily get pulled into other assignments that could contribute to their growth.

I've even observed roles being created around someone's ethnicity, gender, or sexual orientation to advise on cultural issues, connect with community members or customers, etc. There are a couple of problems here: 1) if and when the individual leaves the organization, this knowledge, insight, and expertise leaves with them, and 2) associating a function or practice with ethnicity or gender, etc., minimizes the need for others to learn about it, care about it, or be held accountable for it.

A colleague told me that she worked for a major consumer goods organization that created a multicultural marketing unit. This opened up a number of new and expanded role opportunities for Blacks and Latinx professionals. At some point during a restructure of the marketing department, the organization decided to dissolve this unit; and guess who got caught in the middle? Because these employees had focused on targeted marketing efforts for so long, they hadn't had a chance to develop in other areas and, subsequently, did not qualify for new roles that came out of the restructuring. Pigeonholing might be born out of an attempt to leverage someone's unique insights (intent), but it has also resulted in the stagnation of the career trajectories of specific groups whose members would like to play different roles within the organization (impact).

Since we're talking about it, many DEI officer roles were created because individuals who were Black, Latinx, LGBTQ+, differently abled, etc., were viewed as visible representations of diversity that would bring a credible perspective into the role, at least on the surface. Having life experience and empathy does not necessarily qualify one to move into a DEI role. It may enhance one's insights. But it needs to come along with someone who is able to influence others, create partnerships, be strategic, manage projects, manage people, and navigate cultural differences. Need I go on? I have talked with leaders from several organizations who were hesitant to place a White, heterosexual male in a DEI position because they felt it would meet the ire of their employees. This concern, however, does not negate the need to find someone who has experience and is a well-rounded influencer.

Ironically, while one might assume that DEI officer positions would be dominated by executives of color, according to online source Zippia, the most common ethnicity among Chief Diversity Officers in 2022 was White, making up 76.1% of all CDOs. Comparatively, 7.8% of CDOs were Hispanic or Latinx, 7.7% were Asian, 3.8% were Black or African American, and a mere 0.7% were American Indian and Alaska Native. Less surprisingly, this report shared that in 2022, 54.5% of CDOs were women and 45.5% were men.[13]

To close out this discussion, I strongly believe in the benefit of seeking feedback on whether there are disconnects between one's intentions and the perceived impact. Getting this perspective from an external partner who is not "swimming in the same pond" as you can provide immense value.

The Power of Networks and Partnerships

"If you are unsure of what to do in a situation, how to engage others, how not to offend . . . ask somebody. Leverage your networks, those within your

circle, but more importantly, those outside your comfortable circle of friends and colleagues. We. Learn. From. Difference. Period. If everyone you solicit input from agrees with your original point of view, you need to keep soliciting."

This is the mindset that represents my view on the value and power of internal and external partnerships and networks.

I remember the first time that I went to the National Black MBA conference with other employees from my organization. We were putting on workshops as well as sponsoring a recruiting booth. I was amazed at how many Black professionals were at the conference. I think there were over 5,000 attendees at the time, representing every profession from accountant to investment manager to Chief Financial Officer. Attendees were there to hear about employment opportunities as well as offer their insights in various workshops, and more importantly to network. It was a productive, learning, and festive event that I have continued to sponsor in my role as DEI officer. At the time I thought, "Why isn't our leadership here?" I would regularly hear that "we can't find anyone with the skills or experience we need." I'm looking around. There are probably 1,000 people, at minimum, who have the skills, experience, and aptitude to take on any role for which we would be hiring. This is the power of working through professional associations and conferences.

More Partnership Opportunities

There are so many other examples of partnership opportunities. I'll expand on a few more here.

DEI Councils

Given DEI officers are often a department of one, they have to leverage through many others to get the work done. DEI councils are often structured to provide a forum for oversight over DEI initiatives. You will typically have representation from across the organization at different levels and from different regions. Those participating can speak to the nuanced issues and needs that their business units or locations face. There may be term limits every couple of years to refresh the composition. These councils address strategies, review policies, and also provide an opportunity for development around DEI for their constituents. While you may have multiple layers within the organization represented, from individual contributors to C-suite staff, I have also seen councils that are only comprised of senior level business unit leads. There also might be multiple councils within an organization.

Internal Employee Network Groups

Employee Network Groups or Business Resource Groups are another way the DEI officer can get work done in a distributive manner. These groups benefit the members as they are structured to address the unique needs and interests of specific demographic groups. They provide mentoring, professional development, and a safe space for members to discuss organizational challenges. The members benefit the organization by bringing their insights and worldview to various business problems and opportunities. Members serve as "boots on the ground" at conferences, helping with recruiting and interviewing. They will also often assist with reviewing company policies and practices, participate in focus groups, and plan events for the entire organization to increase employee engagement.

During the course of my career, several of my employers and clients have sponsored Business Resource Groups that provide a forum for women, LGBTQ+, Blacks, Asian/Pacific Islanders, Latinx, Veterans, Differently Abled, Middle Eastern, and North African employees. The engagement and contribution of these groups to business goals has been nothing short of *amazing*!

Now I realize there is some controversy around Employee Network Groups. Some may think that they actually reinforce divisiveness within organizations. But most organizations who sponsor these groups enable anyone from within the organization to join them. This results in a blend of individuals coming together who match a specific demographic, as well as allies to these groups, and those who are interested in learning more about the group. Executive sponsorship is often a requirement for these groups to exist, and this serves to provide a development opportunity for senior leaders. It enables company leadership to become more in tune with the challenges, insights, and desired career goals that individuals within the group have. In turn, the senior leader can provide line-of-sight to the big picture initiatives that the business is embarking upon. This networking makes these partnerships a win-win for those sponsoring them, for those participating in them, for the DEI officer, and for the organization as a whole.

Advocacy Organizations and Nonprofits

There are local and national advocacy organizations and nonprofits whose missions are to help their member companies and the general business community enhance diversity, equity, and inclusion. For example, there is the Urban League, the Anti-Defamation League, Leadership Greater Chicago, which is replicated in other major centers throughout the United States, Chicago United, the Executive Leadership Council, and numerous others. These organizations help address workforce issues and the pipeline of talent; they provide inclusive leadership training and mentoring. Organizations like the National Minority Supplier Development Council also provide services that help organizations expand opportunities to businesses and suppliers from diverse cultural groups. These nonprofits focus on community empowerment and social justice endeavors as well. During the course of my career, I have sat on the advisory board of many of these nonprofit organizations and can attest to the value they bring to corporations.

Industry Consortiums and Roundtables

There are also consortiums that have been formed within industries. I'll make reference to the financial industry in Chicago. A group of banks—commercial, investment management, and personal—have formed a consortium. The Financial Services Pipeline recognizes that it only hurts the industry to poach from each other when looking to fill positions with candidates from diverse backgrounds; and so they have collaborated on ways to source and develop talent in a way that is a win-win for all institutions involved.

Industry roundtables serve a similar purpose. Instead of hoarding ideas and best practices that your company has implemented, these forums enable individuals in similar professions, such as DEI officers, or change management professionals, to connect. Representing their different companies, members share challenges and tested strategies in monthly or quarterly forums. I have often been invited to participate in these meetings and have seen, firsthand, the energy and engagement of all involved.

Search Firms, Pipeline Development Organizations, and Academia

There are industry-specific organizations that help source and develop talent in specialized areas like technology and healthcare. Organizations that have been around for decades, like Inroads and I.C.Stars, help with creating summer internships and mentoring programs for high school and college students. Menttium and other organizations help businesses match high-potential talent with external mentors.

Search firms can be leveraged particularly when you keep hearing that "we can't find any." Organizations can require the search firms they con-tract with to bring in a diverse slate of candidates who meet initial screening criteria. These firms have tentacles globally and can often quickly place candidates in front of an organization. Search firms are also often engaged in conducting research on DEI trends. These White papers and reports are quite valuable for DEI officers who may not have the internal resources to take on this activity.

Attending recruiting fairs and establishing relationships with colleges and universities that serve specific populations can also help with identifying talent. There are numerous academic organizations I and my colleagues have built partnerships with including Historically Black Colleges and Universities (HBCUs), the Hispanic Association of Colleges and Universities (HACUs), and Tribal Colleges and Universities (TCUs).

External Consultants, Coaches, Facilitators, and Speakers

Bringing in external consultants as partners often helps provide additional resources and or expertise in an organization's early phases of implementing DEI. Where this is really needed is when organizations begin to do things differently, like lunch and learn sessions or hosting candid conversations around traumatic and culture-related societal events. I say this because I always get the question from leaders on what they can do to respond to a recent hate crime, mass shooting, or other incident within the community. The initial response from organizations is to provide counseling resources for employees who would like to discuss this and/or seek mental health solutions. I also hear from many employees and managers that they would like to have a conversation at their upcoming staff meetings. While this might, in concept, sound like a good idea, I would advise against it unless you have a facilitator who is very well-trained and understands group dynamics. A great facilitator knows how to set the stage, set the tone, create ground rules for participation, and guide the discussion. It's very important to be clear about the objectives of the meeting and sometimes the goal is just to allow people to tell their stories or have their say.

This needs to be someone who can pay attention to the cues in the room, when people speak and or don't speak, someone who can guide the conversation when it becomes very emotional or goes off track. Good facilitators can assist those attending, share in a respectful manner, especially in polarized groups, and leave feeling that the session was worthwhile. They are aware of their impact on others and can sense the impact that individuals within the group are having on each other. Facilitation of difficult conversations involves a complex set of skills that are honed over time. So, the next time you think it's a good idea to facilitate a challenging conversation yourself, think again.

In sum, I would say that for every organizational need that can't be addressed internally or where there are not sufficient resources, there is an external partner with whom the organization can collaborate. Now I realize there's a cost to doing so, and that organizations need to prioritize expenditures, but the return on investment in partnerships is priceless.

Tactical Tools/Considerations

Throughout this chapter, I have mentioned several approaches, tools, tips, and cautions that should be kept in mind as organizations embark upon building the requisite skills needed for advancing DEI efforts. To round out those suggestions, here is a brief list of considerations.
Individuals can:

- Advocate for yourself, highlight relevant skills developed outside of the workplace, and show how they are transferrable.
- Engage in self-reflection when you believe you have offended a coworker.
- Seek feedback when you are not sure.
- Build social capital by identifying informal mentors and individuals who can sponsor you.
- Join community organizations, nonprofit boards, and internal committees and Employee Resource Groups to hone leadership, project management skills, and build cross-cultural competency.

Organizational leaders and practitioners can:

- Conduct an assessment to get baseline metrics on your leadership team's level of cross-cultural competency.
- Create development plans for building cross-cultural competency across the organization.
- Create cross-cultural mentoring partnerships to spark Ah Ha moments and learning.
- Create a strategic partnership plan that aligns with business goals and DEI goals.
- Participate in DEI and industry roundtables.
- Review the impact of various policies and practices on varying demographic groups.
- Enable employees to provide anonymous feedback on management practices, career growth challenges, and the work environment.

4

Did You See Something? Bystanders and Allies

Being the Change

I have so many personal stories and there are so many incidents I can speak to that have happened during the course of my lifetime that provide examples of the unbelievable ways in which humans can observe inhumane offenses against others and not respond. We can join in on offensive and violent group behavior and not feel guilt.

But to our credit as human beings, I've also seen individuals step up to the plate and demonstrate courageous behaviors in the midst of observing an injustice to another person. There are many societal examples of this and just as many occurrences in the corporate setting.

This chapter will present a number of scenarios and speak to my insights along with proposed theories on understanding bystander and group behaviors. I will start with a personal reflection that has a redeemable outcome; but beware, all of the stories shared here may not. They may spark rage in some, disbelief in others. My hope is that they will spark Ah Ha moments that will lead to a shift in some of your perspectives, and ultimately a change in behaviors. Change starts with you!

Be the change you wish to see in the world.

Flighty Experiences

My wife and I were getting on a flight to Connecticut to see our goddaughter, Monica Nia—Miss Illinois—compete in the Miss America pageant. We were sitting in first class, and the flight was full. One of the last passengers to get on the plane was a woman from India. She finally made it to her seat. The woman behind her kept hitting the back of her seat, because, as it turned out, the seat was broken and kept leaning back on the woman. The flight attendant who was a Black woman saw this and said "I'll take care of this. We will find her another seat." This was not good enough for the woman.

She proceeds to hurl spit into the woman's hair in front of her. The flight attendant, seeing this, calls up front to describe the situation. I can hear the entire conversation. The flight attendant she called was Black as well. They appeared to be struggling with what to do, reasoning whether they should escalate the situation. I suspect it was because the woman who complained and then assaulted the Indian woman was White.

So, I decided to intervene. I said, "Follow protocol. Do not defray." I also told the flight attendant that the Indian woman could have my seat in first class. When they brought her to my seat, the woman was so embarrassed and looked like she feared for her life. She actually leaned into my chest as I tried to solace and comfort her—to be an ally for her in a moment where she felt all alone.

The flight attendant proceeded to take the frightened woman to wash the saliva out of her hair, and I could see that it was clearly saliva. It was a sticky mess. Still nothing else had been done. So, I decided to intervene again. I said, "This woman should be kicked off the plane. She assaulted someone. Follow protocol. Do not defray." Unbeknownst to them, I had a close relationship with the CEO of the airline as I was one of their Airline's Diversity Council members. The pilot on this particular flight was Latino; he was also a new crew member; and he didn't suggest to do anything differently either. I said again, "You all need to follow protocol!"

I then told the crew, "Google my name and you will see that I am speaking from a place of authority." They eventually called the Chicago police to come to escort the White woman from the plane. Two hours later two police officers arrive. The gate agent went back to the woman's seat and escorted her to the front of the plane to deboard. I heard her say, "I didn't spit on her. I was simply opening my can of pop and it got in her hair."

She held up her hand and I could not help but notice she was holding a bottle versus a can, and that let me know right then and there she wasn't telling the truth. She had no remorse.

A White male police officer heard the story and got very emotional. He led with, "She did what? She better be glad she didn't do that to me. I would have knocked her out. Do you know what it takes to spit on somebody?!" For him, it was unheard of for someone to treat another human being that way.

The Black female police officer with him took a different approach and said, "Well now wait a minute. We don't know if this is true. We've got to get both sides of the story." Additionally, another woman passenger on the plane who was White had come forward to say, "Look I witnessed the whole thing, but I don't want to get in the middle of this. I don't want you to mention my name. But I did see this woman spit on this poor woman here."

Eventually they escorted the woman off the plane so that we could continue with our flight. I remembered that the CEO asked that if any members on the Diversity Council noticed anything on his aircraft that didn't seem right that action could be taken. So, with the flight crew's acknowledgment, I took the speaker phone and said, "Ladies and Gentlemen, I am apologizing on behalf of the pilot, the crew, and the president of this airline for this inconvenience. But I want to ask you a question. What if the scenario you just witnessed happened to your mother, sister, or daughter? Wouldn't you have wanted someone to intervene, step up, and lean into the conversation." I was met with deer in the headlight gazes and half open jaws. However, when we landed in Connecticut, several people came up to me and thanked me for intervening and being an ally. Yet they were unwilling to do the same.

I question why the crew of color hesitated in following protocol with this woman. But it's not surprising as they probably viewed her as being a person of privilege and were willing to let her sidestep this infraction, this assault, this offense to another human. The dynamics do not always play out that way; however when they do, I am reminded of how our socialization often results in us ignoring the evidence in front of us.

> *If you are neutral in situations of injustice, you have chosen the side of the oppressor. If an elephant has its foot on the tail of a mouse, and you say that you are neutral, the mouse will not appreciate your neutrality."*
> —Archbishop Desmond Tutu

The Bystander Effect

What behavior can be used to help us understand why people stand by and watch but don't respond to abuse, offense, and assaults they see happening in front of them? To begin to dissect this I will refer to the literature on bystanders. A bystander has been described in many ways. The bystander effect refers to an urgent or emergency situation in which people who witness it do not offer to help. It is typically influenced by current group dynamics, group think, and deindividuation, which simply means that no one person feels accountable, especially when they are with a group of other people, such as a crowd. When we think of bystanders as it relates to cultural events like racism, sexism, homophobia, and others, the bystander is someone who sees or knows about the incident, is not the target, and often is not directly involved. They choose to do nothing, which in essence supports the behavior they see.

And why do people choose to do nothing? As mentioned, being part of a group lessens the feeling of accountability. But it also could be because the situation is so intense or there's a perceived danger in it where people are afraid of becoming a target themselves. Individuals may not want to draw attention to themselves because they might either fear backlash or reprisal from the group in which they are in the midst. It could also be that people just don't know what to say or do. Perhaps they think something should be done, but they're not quite sure what is appropriate. And then there are probably a number of scenarios where the individual who is observing actually has a bias or prejudice against the victimized person or, at minimum, a lack of empathy for what they are going through.

The bystander effect gained national media attention from the Kitty Genovese case. This took place in 1964 in New York City, where a 28-year-old woman was brutally attacked in an alley, just steps away from her apartment. She was screaming out loudly, but the close to 40 people who heard her did nothing. No one attempted to intervene and save her. It was mentioned that one call was made to the police, but the police dismissed it as a domestic dispute and so did not arrive to help.

I realize that sometimes people go into a semi state of shock when they are in a tense situation that requires giving support, but there are certainly a few things that can be done. At minimum someone can use their phone and call 911. If it is not a situation where physical harm is a threat, they can share their observations and feelings on what they see happening, try to comfort the person who has been targeted, and seek assistance from others who are around them. Observers have more credit than they often give themselves to take some action to either draw attention to what is happening, get others involved, and or stop what is taking place.

Failure to respond to the cries for help from someone who is experiencing abuse or offense is bad enough. What makes it worse is that there is research that suggests that there are racial disparities in how individuals respond. For example, in a research study involving White female college students, it was found that their intent to intervene when a situation suggested that someone was at risk for sexual assault was significantly less if it was suggested that the woman who was being assaulted was Black versus White.[1] We've all heard of incidents in the media where someone blames the victim saying, "she should have known not to wear that," or "why would she go up to his room in the first place." Some of these were reasons given across the studies that were done.

What's even more concerning are the studies done in the medical field that suggest individuals experiencing a medical emergency or needing CPR are less likely to get assistance if they are Black. In one study that looked at bystander support during medical emergencies on U.S. streets, bystanders provided help but only about 1 in 39 patients (2.5%) received support and for Blacks this was less than a percentage point. It was also found that the most disadvantaged counties were least likely to receive bystander support.[2] So, we haven't even gotten to the workplace yet; but you can anticipate how this pattern would most likely trickle into this setting for employees living in and commuting back and forth from under-resourced communities.

Another study published in a research report by the Brookings Institute looked at bystander intervention on social media. This research study focused on hate speech and cyberbullying related to race and racism. They looked at and were able to categorize discussion threads under stereotyping, scapegoating, accusations of reverse racism, and echo chambers. Analyzing over two million tweets and posts from Twitter and Reddit from 2020, the authors examined the effectiveness of bystander strategies used to combat racism. The findings were that only one in six Twitter (now "X") discussions and slightly less than 40% of Reddit discussions featured any bystander action. When they did find bystander intervention strategies, these included call outs, insults or mocking, attempts to educate or provide evidence, and content moderation.[3] Social media has augmented the view into polarized viewpoints on racism and White supremacy. Many actions have occurred in reaction to the Black Lives Matter movement where hate speech and cyberbullying are done by those who are able to mask their identities. The authors suggest that this is similar to the use of KKK hoods in the past.

Go Back to Africa!

I remember being a part of a panel discussion at a CEO conference. I was the only Black person on the panel. A White CEO in the audience stood up and said, "This question is for Tyronne. I don't understand the Black Lives Matter movement. If Blacks feel that Black lives don't matter in this country, why don't they just go back to Africa?"

Everybody in the crowd just gasped. And I had an out-of-body moment. I got out of my seat and walked to the edge of the stage and said, "You cannot return stolen merchandise. There is no policy for returning Blacks who were kidnapped, hoodwinked, brought over on ships in chains, thrown into the ocean, hung from trees, and beaten to submission!" I then asked, "By show of hands, how many of the White people in the audience would trade places with a Black man? You have to understand we are starting from a deficit and of no choice of our own. Why would I go back to Africa? I can't even trace my roots back to Africa. I am an American who happens to be Black." I then elaborated on the deficit that Black Americans are affected by, sharing the following example that I borrowed from Dr. Margaret Burroughs of Operation Push.

"Imagine playing a Monopoly board for 450 rounds. Capturing my experience as a Black man in America, I've gone around the board 450 times, and never had the chance to collect $200. As a White man, you've collected $200 each time you have gone around the board, and as you did so you bought property, railroads, and utilities. The moment I collect my first $200, in the 451st round, I land on your property—Boardwalk—and because I don't have quite enough money to pay you, I go to jail. I roll the dice again and I get out of jail. I then land on your railroad, and I can't afford to pay you, because I don't have any money, and so then have to go back to jail. But we had the same chance to go around the board, right? That's equality. But given your head start and historical advantage, equity does not exist.

"Now, imagine this dynamic playing out for the Black community for the past 450 years. We have to look at the systems that are created that are holding people back, the judicial system, the legal system, the penal system, sub-par healthcare, limited access to financial resources, disproportionate interest rates on home loans, red lining. The list goes on and on. My point—Blacks will never reach parity with our White wealthy counterparts."

This created an Ah Ha moment for the man who asked the question as well as for others in the audience. Eventually, this CEO and I became good friends. I conducted the Intercultural Development Inventory (IDI) assessment with him and his team to help them gauge where they were on cross cultural competency. I learned that he was in an interracial marriage and had biracial children; yet this was the man who challenged the Black Lives Matter movement.

He wasn't aware. He couldn't be sympathetic or empathetic. He just saw that "this is America; and if you don't like it, leave it." But this America was built on the backs of Blacks, individuals who have received pennies on the dollar for their contributions.

Construction Site Shenanigans

Speaking of "built on the backs of," allow me to fast forward to a more recent "indecent." I am serving as a DEI consultant to a group of primes or prime contractors and subcontractors on a construction site. As I was interviewing some of the employees, I learned about a couple of questionable occurrences from crew members. The first outlandish report was that a noose was found on the construction site! The second was that a group of White men had lifted a Black woman, using a Porta Potty, 20 feet in the air . . . as a joke!

Not so funny, and not so uncommon. My consulting colleagues have shared similar stories of nooses appearing in plant locker rooms and related offenses. In the scenario I shared, these occurrences speak to how easily group behavior can get out of control and contribute to a toxic work environment. Many White construction workers who have been in the industry for 25 to 30 years have never worked alongside a Black person. Some are three generations into construction and are now in a situation where they have to work with a Black person or woman who is equally or more qualified. They are having difficulties accepting this.

So, they are finding ways to make it tough for the women who have entered into this industry—loading them down unnecessarily with tools that would put a strain on anyone's body. This is a form of bullying or gaslighting that is occurring that is rooted in bias, fear, and corrupt collusion.

Social Identity and Group Behavior

Corrupt behaviors, perpetrated in groups, can be explained but not excused. Taking a deeper dive into groups, how they are formed, and how they affect our behavior is warranted here. This will help us think through strategies that can diminish bystander effects, or inaction, and create more courageous and compassionate actions.

When we think of the many types of groups that exist, there are some that are structured and it is clear that we belong to them. This could be a civic/social organization like a fraternity, a work team, your family, your community, a cultural group, a political group, etc. You feel a sense of affinity with the group members. You may share the same values, background, and ideology. You will tend to engage with some groups more than others.

There are also groups that you are a part of with whom you would not necessarily self-identify. Consider the passengers who were on the flight with me in the example at the beginning of this chapter. They may see themselves as a group, if you define it loosely. What they have in common is that they are all on a flight and going toward a similar destination. But there is no significant interdependence on each other or need to interact.

This could quickly change, though, in an emergency situation. For example, if there was the appearance of a hijacker or some dangerous threat on the plane, the passengers would go from being just a collection of individuals to being a group that needs to rely on each other in order to remain calm, de-escalate the situation, or take some other form of action. I can relate this situationally formed group to the flight that I was on. There was an incident on the plane that we all observed; however I assume, by the lack of action, that there was not a felt need to engage. I felt just the opposite, however. I felt there was a need for collective engagement, perhaps not by every single person on the plane, but at least by those in charge of the plane's safety, that is, the flight crew.

Let's delve into how strongly one identifies with a group. Research suggests that that there are a lot of psychological and social reasons for identifying with certain groups. In general, most people want to maintain a high sense of self-esteem or self-concept. Some of that is their individual mindset. But part of it is the value assigned to the groups with whom one identifies.

Otherness

If we look at social comparison theories, we would tend to want the groups with whom we identify to have a higher status than other groups. This is where the concept of "otherness" comes in and why it is often perceived as a deficit of sorts. In sum, we make comparisons between different groups that we feel we are a part of and those that we feel we are not. We want to view the groups that we are part of more positively, which often leads us to, unconsciously if not deliberately, view other groups negatively.

Given that the groups with whom we identify help raise our self-esteem, we also do not want to demonstrate any behaviors that might cause us to be ostracized from the group. We go along to get along; and this is what can lead to dysfunctional, harmful, or negligent group behavior. One example is the 2021 insurrection at the nation's capital.

The literature also tells us that those participating in crowds and mobs feel less of a need to evaluate the appropriateness of their behaviors, because being a part of a crowd provides a sense of anonymity and lack of accountability. Social contagion sparks others within the group to go along with the group's behaviors and norms whether they be positive or outlandish.

Group-driven behaviors can become more noticeable and polarizing when we consider otherness and those who we do not consider to be a part of our group. If we think back to how our brain operates, when it notices something different, it has a tendency to overreact, going into survival mode. This might manifest as fear, distrust, resentment, or skepticism. This can lead to power struggles and competition over resources if members from different groups view things from a win-lose mindset. Generally, when there is more exposure and interaction with individuals from different groups, these unconscious fears, etc., are able to subside.

Building Empathy

In fact, one of the major strategies for helping different groups build appreciation and empathy for each other is to design forums and opportunities for them to engage more or experience the world or work setting through the lens of someone else. Along with building appreciation and empathy, this tactic enables participants to challenge their stereotypes, learn more about other worldviews, and better understand their own worldview. In the work setting, cross-cultural mentoring relationships help foster this as does participation on cross-disciplinary work teams.

There have been a couple of landmark interventions that were done to create this empathy starting with a younger population. One of the more famous ones was led by Jane Elliott and highlighted in the short documentary *A Class Divided*.[4] Shortly after the assassination of Martin Luther King, Jr. in 1968, a third grade teacher in Riceville, Iowa, decided she wanted her students to learn what it felt like to be discriminated against. She constructed an experiment where she divided the class in two based on their eye color. She told the class on the first day of the experiment that the group with the blue eyes was superior to those with the brown eyes, that they were more intelligent, better behaved, and performed better. She also made the brown eyes group wear a collar around their necks to draw attention to them. What she witnessed was extraordinary. The behavior of the blue eyes toward the brown eyes was aggressive, mean, and condescending. The brown eyes walked around feeling dejected and could not focus well on their assignments.

The next day, Jane Elliott let the class know that she had it wrong and that the brown eyes were actually superior to the blue eyes. They switched roles and collars, and what she found was more self-confidence demonstrated by the brown eyes as well as more aggressive behavior toward the blue eyes. Again, her experiment showed students would actually perform better if they were part of the group deemed to be superior.

By the end of the experiment, when Elliott indicated that no one was better than anybody else and that the blue eyes could take their collars off, everybody was relieved. This is just a short synopsis, but it points to how believing you are part of a superior group or inferior group can actually change your behaviors. She knew that this would impress the students in her class, and in fact reconnected with them after they became adults to see if there were any long-term impacts.

She found out that this intervention had remarkably influenced the thoughts and the direction that her students followed as they moved into adulthood. They had more empathy for other ethnic groups and were involved in activities that demonstrated that. She has replicated this experiment with adults in organizational settings, as well, and has observed similar findings. The silver lining from these interventions is the empathy that it helps build along with the opportunity for self-reflection on how we automatically make positive or negative associations based on group membership.

I strongly believe that building empathy within our youth is the key to building a society that can appreciate and embrace difference. Children are very impressionable and internalize what they see from figures of authority in their households, in their schools, and in the media. For children already living in households that espouse hate and prejudice, this will be a challenging journey. Our institutions need to continue creating venues for acceptance of those not like us. This is a societal and systemic issue, yet each "Jane Elliott" who chooses to be an ally and advocate, can be a force for change.

It takes a village to raise a child.

—African Proverb

Other ways to minimize tension and distrust across group is to introduce a superordinate goal that both groups want to achieve and that requires their interdependent actions. Sometimes natural disasters bring disparate communities together. We saw the nation come together, somewhat, when we had to address the COVID-19 pandemic. Quickly reducing the fatalities and solving this global problem became a superordinate goal. Local, state, national, and global entities collaborated to do so. In the midst of it, we still saw finger pointing and blaming but everyone wanted to find a solution.

Superordinate goals often bring siloed teams together in the workplace. Convening crossfunctional task forces that may be brought together to help strategize the best way to move forward after a merger or perhaps address ways to be more innovative or planet-focused as new consumer products are developed is one approach I've observed. It is a way to enable employees to hear and appreciate the unique value of different function-based perspectives. Conferences that unite different Employee Resource Groups around a specific organizational challenge or opportunity facilitate this as well. The Ah Ha or light bulb moments that I have often seen in these forums lead to more empathy and ultimately to more action and care.

Ally in Flight

I remember another flight that I was on. I was sitting in first class. A young African American male was in the seat right behind first class. He talked the entire flight! The poor woman next to him at one point said, "I'm just going to close my eyes for a while," but he kept on talking. He was so excited and nervous. I overheard him say this was the first time he had flown. Once the plane landed and we had pulled up to the gate, he jumped out of his seat and ran toward the door. Well, you know the other passengers in first class with me were quite annoyed by this and one man decided to chastise him. I nipped this in the bud, stepped in, pulled the brother aside and said, "Son, listen. There's a protocol to this. Let me walk you through it." And I explained to him what it was.

He said, "I'm so sorry. I just didn't know what I didn't know." I acknowledged this and asked him to allow me to help him. We walked out of the plane together. As we were heading down to the baggage carousel, three people who were on the plane came over to me and said, "I love the way that you helped that young man! I love the way you stepped in for him because it could have turned out to be a very ugly situation."

I extended a ride into the city to this young man, saying, "I don't know how you were planning on getting there but I'm going to give you my driver's information so that you can let the person you are meeting downtown know your whereabouts; and you can also Google me to see who I am." I wanted to create psychological safety for him. We talked the entire way. I learned a lot about him, his profession, and his family.

I like to share this story because it is an example of how you can be an ally to someone who may not be behaving appropriately as well as stand up for someone who's being victimized.

The Power of Allyship

Given the inequities that marginalized groups are facing at a systemic level and the fact that there is little chance of reaching parity with their White counterparts, I feel it is important to elaborate on the role of allyship. Allyship has been described in many ways. What resonates with me is that it is a process versus a status that someone achieves. It requires learning, re-evaluating, advocating, and helping amplify the voices of those who are marginalized within our society and within the workplace. It requires those in the role to actively listen, to be supportive in the moment and long-term in order to create more equitable outcomes for those who are underrepresented. It is a continual process of taking courageous action wherever you might be—on a plane or in a Zoom meeting.

Within DEI it involves taking an active role to ensure that all members within the workforce are included, supported, sponsored, seen, and heard. Allyship can take the form of wearing a rainbow flag pin on your lapel or hanging one outside of your door. This helps contribute to the organizational culture. It can extend to more visible actions like speaking out for or against a principle, marching alongside of, pulling others into the conversation, acknowledging "hidden figures," and celebrating successes.

When I reflect on the need to celebrate the successes and accomplishments of those from marginalized groups, my dear friend, Xernona Clayton comes to mind. Xernona Clayton is the founder, president, and

CEO of the Trumpet Awards Foundation, and creator and executive producer of the Foundation's Trumpet Awards. The Trumpet Awards is a prestigious event highlighting African American accomplishments and contributions in many different fields. This award ceremony sounds the trumpet for many individuals on a global stage. Initiated in 1993 by Turner Broadcasting, the Trumpet Awards has been televised annually and distributed to over 185 countries.

Clayton herself has been a pioneer in the media industry and in the Civil Rights Movement. She has received numerous awards and recognitions for her active involvement. Pulling from her online bio she is *"the driving force behind the International Civil Rights Walk of Fame at the Martin Luther King Jr. National Historic Site in Atlanta. Clayton worked undercover for the Chicago Urban League investigating employment discrimination before moving to Atlanta in 1965 to organize events for the Southern Christian Leadership Conference (SCLC). She developed a deep friendship with Dr. King and his wife, Coretta Scott King. In 1966, Clayton also coordinated the activities of Atlanta's African American physicians in Doctors' Committee for Implementation. That project helped force the desegregation of all hospital facilities in Atlanta. As a journalist, Clayton wrote a column for the Atlanta Voice, and in 1967, she became the first Black person in the South to host a regularly scheduled prime-time television talk show."*

Xernona Clayton is an inspiring ally who continues providing visible support to others and who uses her position and power to advance equity.

The power of allyship is very well stated in a 2020 article published in the *Harvard Business Review* on "How to Be a Better Ally." The authors state:

> *We view allyship as a strategic mechanism used by individuals to become collaborators, accomplices, and coconspirators who fight injustice and promote equity in the workplace through supportive*

personal relationships and public acts of sponsorship and advocacy. Allies endeavor to drive systemic improvements to workplace policies, practices, and culture. When you witness discrimination, don't approach the victim later to offer sympathy. Give him or her your support in the moment. Especially if you have positional authority or status, you should use a "pull" approach: In meetings, ask very specific questions of people whose contributions and expertise are often overlooked or devalued, so that alpha White men and their bravado can't hog the floor. It also helps to "decenter" yourself.[5]

While allyship has been talked about extensively in the workplace, we can trace its roots back through centuries. Historically, there have been many allies supporting major societal movements. I highlighted the works of Xernona Clayton. Building on that example, we know the power of allyship and advocacy was also evident when Jewish citizens, White men and women, walked alongside Blacks during the Civil Rights era. They realized that what harms one harms us all. What benefits one of us should benefit all of us.

There is a risk when one becomes very visible as an ally for controversial movements like the Civil Rights, Black Lives Matter, or LGBTQ+ movements. White citizens like Anne Braden, James Reeb, and Vilola Liuzzo who advocated for civil rights often faced serious repercussions including ostracization from their communities, accusations of sedition and communism, job loss, physical violence, and death. Allyship requires courage and commitment.

Demonstrating allyship in the workplace can take on many forms. But we should remember that the workplace often extends outside the brick-and-mortar walls or Zoom rooms in which we operate. Boarding a plane to go to a work conference provides an opportunity for allyship. While the length of the interaction you may have with an individual may be short, it may be just what they need for support in the moment, to inspire them or help their voice or concerns be heard.

I will often exhibit what I consider to be allyship in meetings. When I see that someone is talking over someone else or taking credit for someone else's work, I will intervene and say something like, "Sharon, didn't you say the same thing" or "Don't you have a similar thought around that? I remember we talked about this the other day." Or if we haven't heard from Sharon in the meeting, I might say something like, "Sharon what do you think? I know you have a lot of thoughts around this that you've shared with me." This is the language I use particularly for individuals who might be a bit shy or introverted or feel that their opinion doesn't matter. It is a way to amplify their voice, to invite them into the conversation.

Showing Support During Catastrophic Events

During the writing of this book another tragic event surfaced that shook the global community. On October 7, 2023, Hamas militants stormed into nearby Israeli towns and executed a surprise attack during a major Jewish holiday. Hundreds were killed or abducted. This led to the declaration of war in the Middle East. As I write this, in less than a week since this attack there has been cumulative violence, destruction, and a disrespect for humanity.

Employers know that individuals are shaken to the core watching these developments, and that they bring their fears, worries, and loss to the workplace. We are seeing occurrences like this more often than not. Within the same year, the war between Russia and Ukraine is still ongoing, mass shootings are occurring almost weekly, and natural disasters like wildfires, torrential rains, and hurricanes are displacing families and impacting lives.

As the lead for DEI, I am often involved in conversations about how to address our employees and the broader community. The issues surrounding these tragedies are very complex and cannot be turned around by private industry; but we also cannot simply stand by. Companies can show their allyship, support, and compassion in many ways. Some of the leading practices for doing so include:

- Sending out a communication right away that acknowledges these events. Let employees and the general public know that the company views this as a serious issue. This communication should indicate that leadership is deeply impacted by what has happened, is mourning alongside the community, and will do what it can to bring aid and support. This correspondence should be crafted by a communications specialist and reviewed for sensitivity by employees from diverse backgrounds.
- Listening and holding space. While there is no perfect way to respond in times of crisis, one of the ways that you can show care is by checking in on your colleagues and peers and letting them know that you're here to support them.
- Encouraging well-being breaks. Employers should anticipate a range of emotions as updates on the situation are received. They should encourage colleagues to step away from their work, if needed, for a quiet moment of reflection and the processing of emotions. If feasible, employees should be given more flexibility to work remotely.
- Encouraging employees to utilize Well-being Resources & Employee Assistance Program. Provide links and phone numbers for service providers, Employee Assistance Programs, and to any wellness assessment tools available. Ensure employees that their conversations will be held in confidence.
- Establishing resources for employees' family members, e.g., children. Organizations like ComPsych provide on-demand training to help adults have conversations with their children about world events.

- Helping identify ways for employees to get involved. During times of crisis, employees often want to be able to show their own individual support but may not know how. Leaders can provide lists and links to credible organizations that are accepting donations or volunteer assistance.

Psychological Safety

Creating psychologically safe work environments goes hand in hand with allyship. This term, coined by Kahn in 1990, refers to a person feeling that they can express their ideas, concerns, and take certain risks without the fear of negative consequences to their self-image, status, or career.[6] Psychological safety can be created and supported by an individual as well as by group members within a team. There are many studies that show the benefits of psychologically safe workplaces including those that show a correlation between it and inclusiveness. In a study conducted in 2016 in a Mid-Atlantic teaching hospital, it was found that leader inclusiveness was positively correlated with psychological safety.[7] There also have been studies that show that there are different leadership styles associated with psychological safety. Those that are positively related include the servant leadership style.

Psychological safety is a global phenomenon and also has been shown to promote learning and innovation. This is not surprising as when people feel they are able to perform without fear of reprisal they can focus on being productive and sharing novel ideas. Those who feel psychologically safe were also shown to exhibit greater engagement, organizational citizenship behaviors, and knowledge sharing behaviors or collaboration. So, when you feel you are in a safe environment you are more prone to help others and to pass it forward. This came out of a study conducted in Taiwan in 2021 by Liu and Keller.[8]

In a research study completed in 2023 by Tsikudo, findings showed that the more one felt they were in a psychologically safe environment, the less they felt affected by imposter syndrome.[9] All of the behaviors that have been shown to relate to psychological safety are ones that we as leaders and DEI practitioners know ultimately contribute to work environments where employees are included and feel a sense of belonging and self-efficacy.

A Couple of Caveats

Thus far I have talked about the bystander effect, group identity, allyship, and psychological safety and I trust my readers can see the connection and interdependency of all of these concepts. There are a couple of things I want to share that also relate to group behavior that we need to be mindful of as they have a win-lose nature to them.

Crabs in a Barrell

I've often heard people refer to and use the "crabs in a barrel" or "crabs in a bucket" metaphor to describe how members within one's own group pull down each other because there is either jealousy or a sense of competition. They don't want those within their own group to get ahead. The "crabs in the barrel" metaphor is relevant as it suggests that you don't have to put any kind of lid on the barrel because the crabs won't get out. They will keep pulling each other down so that no one makes it to the top. This might manifest as less than flattering remarks about someone you know is seeking the same promotion opportunity as you.

The crabs in the barrel metaphor might describe behavior within a specific context; and some might argue that they've seen it more in certain minority groups than others. But there is another point of view that suggests that it's not the crabs in the barrel or the individuals that we should be focusing on, it is the barrel itself!

The barrel represents the systemic issues that create inequities in the first place. It is the environment in which the crabs live that is confined and restricting. We can liken this to underresourced communities, inadequate schooling systems, limited access to financial resources, abuses from law enforcement and the penal system. In the workplace, it can be seen in the limited opportunities to advance and a culture of tokenism where there is a threshold for how many Blacks or women, for example, we feel comfortable having at the senior levels of our organization.

Considering the environment and all of the systemic barriers in place, focusing on the "crabs" is misdirected energy. I say this so that the next time this example is used to explain group behavior, it is looked at more holistically.

Modern Day Stockholm Syndrome

Another phenomenon that is worth mentioning is one where those who are in an underrepresented group or disadvantaged group align with those who are oppressing them. We can compare this to what has been called Stockholm Syndrome. Stockholm Syndrome is a psychological condition that is observed when a victim of abuse, discrimination, etc., identifies and bonds positively with those who are abusing or oppressing them. The syndrome was identified in 1973 by psychiatrist Nils Bejerot after an attempted bank robbery in Stockholm, Sweden. The bank robbery resulted in a hostage situation that lasted for six days where four bank employees were taken captive. To make a long story short, the hostages were threatened, mistreated, and abused; however, somewhere along the line they developed sympathy for those who had captured them. This resulted in them refusing to talk to or cooperate with the police once they were freed and able to testify.[10]

This story and phenomenon makes me think of those individuals who align with their oppressors now. We have called them everything from

Uncle Toms to sell-outs. We can see examples in politics, in our justice system, and in the media. I won't name names, but will give one example from a TV show that was popular in the 1980s, *Designing Women*.

If you are not familiar with the show or its characters, you can refer to the episode called "The Rowdy Girls."[11] In a nutshell, the main characters, three White women, decide they want to enter a talent show and perform as The Supremes. The women were excited about it, and one of them, Suzanne, decided that they needed to put on dark makeup so they would look more like The Supremes. This could be interpreted as a modern-day Blackface. What was disturbing was that a Black male character, Anthony, a friend of the three women, initially balked at the idea but ended up supporting it at the talent show. Two of the women, Julia and Charlene, when they heard the idea, felt that it was disrespectful and inappropriate and refused to do so, but this did not stop Suzanne from moving forward with it and with the support of her Black friend, Anthony. I believe that the writers' intent was to showcase this buffoonery as the show often centered around presenting teachable moments.

What does this have to do with inclusive organizations? For me it is another example of how individuals from underrepresented groups might "go along to get along"—how they might support those who are misguided but belong to a dominant, more privileged group. The impact? This behavior by one group member might discourage other group members who intuitively feel that an injustice is taking place. So, they stand by and not only watch these offenses, their neutrality actually sanctions the behavior. This erodes understanding and fuels confusion for everyone involved. There are many more real examples of this in society today; but today I will not name names.

Instead, I will close this chapter with the reminder that change begins with you and reiterate some of the steps you can take to create more compassion, courage, empathy, and awareness in your work settings.

Do not get lost in a sea of despair. Be hopeful, be optimistic. Our struggle is not the struggle of a day, a week, a month, or a year, it is the struggle of a lifetime. Never, ever be afraid to make some noise and get in good trouble, necessary trouble.

—*John Lewis, 2018*

Tactical Tools/Considerations

In this chapter, I have discussed important aspects of engaging with bystanders and allies. Here are some of the many tools and techniques you can use to build better relationships.
   Individuals can:

- Remember change *always* begins with you. If you want to know what others are feeling, pay attention to how you are feeling—use yourself as a barometer.
- Engage in regular dialogue with individuals who have a different background or ideology. This will enhance understanding and empathy.
- Notice group dynamics in meetings you participate in. Notice who dominates and those who are typically quiet in discussions. Invite others into the discussion by asking for their perspective.
- Notice the reasons you may hesitate from saying something or taking action when there is injustice. Reflect on what you can do differently.
- Volunteer to assist on projects that involve cross-functional teams.

Organizational leaders and practitioners can:

- Sponsor Employee Resource Groups and actively engage with members to better understand their objectives and their challenges.

- Create cross-cultural mentoring partnerships.
- Observe group dynamics and use your voice to ensure that respect, acknowledgment, and inclusion are embedded in team meetings.
- Provide training and resources on allyship and on how to create psychologically safe work environments.
- Actively work toward inclusion of multiple perspectives and free expression.

5

The Many Faces of Power and Privilege

Get to the Back of the Line!

When people are rude to me, discount me because of my color or other assumptions they have made about me, I default to "empathy and compassion." I try to live by example and respond in a way that does not escalate the situation but can be a teachable moment. I know people are often looking for a knee-jerk reaction, but once you go down that road it can be a very dangerous one to travel.

As an example, I remember getting stuck in Seattle around Christmas one year. The flights were delayed because of a late-night storm in Seattle and snowstorm in Chicago. We had already boarded the plane. At some point the crew announced that we were going to get off the plane and that there was another one leaving in 20 minutes. It was at a different terminal, but because of my VIP access privileges the airlines had someone drive me over to the terminal so that I could get on the flight in time.

They drove me right up to the front of the line of passengers waiting to get on the flight and I bet you can guess how this story goes. A White woman in the line shouted out, "Hey where do you think you're going? Get to the back of the line!" Now I can understand someone thinking that I was butting in, even though I had an official escort; but I have to wonder if it had been a White man who had been driven to the front of the line, would the reaction be the same? The assumption was that I didn't belong there. I had no right to advance to the front of the line. So, while I had specific airline privileges, I did not have the appropriate birthright privileges.

Level Setting: Defining Power and Privilege

How ironic that I would use the term level setting as I open up the discussion on power and privilege, because when we look at these phenomena and how they manifest, circumstances are anything but level or even.

Power and privilege are two social constructs that can either promote or prevent exclusion. Power can be defined as the ability to decide who will have access to resources; the capacity to direct or influence the behavior of others, oneself, or the course of events. Privilege is unearned access to resources only readily available to some people as a result of their advantaged social group membership. It refers to the collective advantages that a person can inherit from birth and accumulate over the course of time.

Power and privilege are influenced by a number of factors. A major factor is one's social identity or group in which one is a member. One could be part of an advantaged or disadvantaged group depending on the context:

- **Advantaged or dominant social groups:** Members of dominant social groups are privileged by birth or acquisition who knowingly or unknowingly reap unfair advantage over members of disadvantaged groups. A dominant group has the power to define and name reality, and determine what is normal, real, and correct.
- **Disadvantaged or marginalized social groups:** Members of social identity groups who have less advantage, are marginalized or excluded, and compartmentalized in defined roles. A marginalized group's culture, language, and history are often misrepresented, discounted, or eradicated, and the dominant group culture is imposed.

So, let's take a look at both of these social constructs in detail, how they manifest, harm, and exclude, and how we can use them to create an environment that promotes inclusion, equity, and belonging.

A Deep Dive into the Types of Power

A framework, developed by French and Raven and referenced widely in the industry, describes six types of power that an individual can hold.

1. **Legitimate power** is the power that a person in the organization holds because of their position. A manager who leads a team has certain responsibilities and also the right to delegate tasks to direct reports as well as review their work and give feedback.
2. **Reward power** arises out of the authority that a person has to recognize and reward people for compliance or performance.
3. **Expert power** is demonstrated through the knowledge and expertise that one possesses and is a valued asset in a knowledge economy. Expert power can also serve as a stepping stone for employees to gain legitimate power.
4. **Referent power** is power that is a result of personal attributes you display that engender a certain level of respect and approachability. It is the ability to influence someone because of their admiration, respect, or identification with you.
5. **Coercive power** is that which enables a person to punish others for noncompliance.
6. **Informational power** results from a person's ability to control the information and communication that others need to accomplish something.[1]

It is certainly possible for an individual to have more than one source of power. Someone who has a combination of legitimate, reward, coercive, and informational power can substantially control and influence outcomes and systemic practices. This can contribute to either an inclusive culture or a toxic one filled with inequities.

Power Imbalances

Power can be further understood by highlighting some of the imbalances we see in society if we look at the journey of marginalized groups. For centuries, women and people of color have not been recognized as citizens with full rights within our nation and globally. Women and people of color have been prohibited or discouraged from getting an education, from being able to vote, getting access to healthcare, getting financing, or moving into certain neighborhoods, entering into many jobs and industries, and advancing into leadership positions. These systemic-driven barriers have impacted the health, well-being, and economic status of these two marginalized groups.

In contrast, White males have been in power for centuries across the globe. They have been able to dictate and influence legislation, acquire and accumulate resources. While the situation has improved, the playing field has been uneven for so long, it is difficult to imagine that women and people of color will ever catch up with White males.

One example of a long-standing inequity is the wage gap. According to the Pew Research Center, women make on average 82% of what men earn. This pay gap is much more severe for Black, Latina, and Indigenous women.[2]

Adding to this is the "pink tax," which is the discriminatory pricing policy of inflating the cost of products marketed to women. For example, there would be a higher cost for shavers, deodorant, and other related products designed for women.

Maternity leave policies also create a barrier for women to demonstrate financial equity. Paid time off for maternity leave is limited in many organizations. Given women are the primary caregivers for children, this impacts them as a group more so than men.

Another barrier is referred to as "the broken rung." In a report done by Lean In, only 87 women for every 100 men are promoted from entry level positions into managerial positions. This ratio falls to 82 out of 100 for women of color.[3] This disparity at the first step into management implies that women will not reach parity with men at the managerial level or in senior leadership positions.

In parallel, we are witnessing a phenomenon similar to the Great Resignation where more women in leadership positions are leaving their companies, which is creating a resource and pipeline problem. For every woman at the director level who was promoted to the next level, the report by Lean In suggests that two women directors are choosing to leave their companies.

Leaving a company does not always result in unemployment. This phenomenon is more likely to be prevalent in specific demographic categories.

According to the Bureau of Labor Statistics, in 2022 Black women had the highest rates of unemployment (5.3%), more than double that for White women (2.6%), Latina women had an unemployment rate of 3.4%, and Asian women had a rate of 2.2%. By comparison, the unemployment rate for White men was 2.8%.[4]

While there are several statistics I could mention that point out inequities, I recognize that these are time-based and impacted by factors like a recession, pandemic, and other societal factors. I project that these inequities will continue and be disrupted or show progress only once there is continual systemic level support and accountability. While systemic support has vacillated given factors like the political administration in place, grassroots efforts have been pervasive throughout history, demonstrating that there is power in numbers.

Power in Numbers

One strategy that marginalized groups have leveraged successfully to influence change is through community organizing. There is power in numbers. Galvanizing the power that comes from aligning with similar-minded individuals, who can be in multiple places at different times, or who can convene en mass in marches and boycotts has been an impactful way of bringing injustices to a greater level of awareness. This has influenced changes in policies and legislation. But for as many groups that have coalesced to bring about social justice for underrepresented, or unrecognized groups, there are also those that convene to promote hate, harm, or dismantle policies that would create more equity.

With so many efforts and movements that have occurred during the last century, I will highlight just a few as examples of power in numbers.

Black Power Movement

Many of the major milestones in the Civil Rights Movement took place prior to 1970. But civil rights groups and activism continue to play an important role in the drive for social justice and equality. The growth of the Black Lives Matter movement highlights how many of the issues that were raised during the 1960s have resurfaced or have yet to be reconciled.

The Evolution of the Black Power Movement

The NAACP was created in 1909 by an interracial group consisting of W.E.B. Du Bois, Ida B. Wells-Barnett, Mary White Ovington, and others who were concerned with the challenges and barriers African Americans faced in the aftermath of the 1908 Springfield (Illinois) Race Riot.

In 1957, Martin Luther King, Jr., Charles Steele, and Fred Shuttlesworth established the Southern Christian Leadership Conference (SCLC). The SCLC became a major force in organizing the Civil Rights Movement and based its principles on nonviolence and civil disobedience.

The Greensboro Sit-In took place in 1960. Four Black students from North Carolina Agricultural and Technical College staged this sit-in at a segregated Woolworth's lunch counter. While they did not get served, the event gained national attention and sparked similar nonviolent protests throughout the South. Six months later the four protesters were able to be served at the Woolworth's lunch counter. Student sit-ins became an effective approach for integrating public facilities like libraries, theaters, and swimming pools.

The Student Nonviolent Coordinating Committee (SNCC) was also established in 1960 at Shaw University in Raleigh, North Carolina. It provided Black youth with a visible role and voice in the Civil Rights Movement. The SNCC later grew into a more radical organization, under the leadership of Stokely Carmichael (1966–1967) who coined the phrase "Black Power." He defined it as an assertion of Black pride and "the coming together of Black people to fight for their liberation, by any means necessary."

The Freedom Riders was a group of students who started taking bus trips throughout the South to test out the implementation of new laws that prohibited segregation in interstate travel facilities (including railway and bus stations). These rides often resulted in police arrests and violent protests but raised awareness of the ongoing practices of segregation.

In 1963 about 200,000 individuals traveled to Washington D.C. to participate in the March on Washington, where Martin Luther King, Jr. delivered his famous "I Have a Dream" speech.

The impact of the speech was viewed as a major factor in the passing of the Civil Rights Act of 1964.

The Black Panthers was founded by Huey Newton and Bobby Seale in 1966 in Oakland, California. The group had revolutionary goals based in Black nationalism, socialism, and armed resistance to police brutality. This group rejected the nonviolence principles of mainstream civil rights organizations.

In 1968 James Brown introduced his top charting song "Say it Loud – I'm Black and I'm Proud." This phrase from the song became an inspiring mantra for Black Americans. In the song, Brown addresses racism and the need for Black empowerment.

Fast forward to 2013 and the birth of Black Lives Matter. This movement emerged after George Zimmerman was acquitted of killing teenager Trayvon Martin. The #BlackLivesMatter hashtag was used on social media to express anger at the inequitable treatment of African Americans within the justice system. During this period, many Americans wore hoodies as a symbol of support to this movement, reflecting the hoodie worn by Trayvon Martin.

The Black Lives Matter movement became global with a wider focus on human rights. This was particularly noted after the murder of George Floyd in 2020. After this incident we also saw the surge of corporate statements expressing their recommitment to diversity, equity, and inclusion as a symbol of support to the wider community.

White Power Movement

Except for race, the White power movement is widely diverse. It includes individuals from a range of belief systems: the KKK, neo-Nazis, White separatists, and proponents of White supremacist religious theologies.

Several of these groups operate in the United States and have been active for over a century. White nationalist groups espouse supremacist ideologies that often allege the inferiority of those considered to be non-White.

The Evolution of the White Power Movement

In 1865 in Pulaski, Tennessee, a group of former confederate soldiers established the Ku Klux Klan (KKK). This group represented White southern resistance to the Republican party's Reconstruction Era policies aimed at establishing political and economic equality for African Americans. While Congress passed legislation to control Klan terrorism, the organization was able to influence the reestablishment of White supremacy through the Democratic party's victories in state legislature across the South in the 1870s. The KKK is active today.

In 1958, Robert H.W. Welch, Jr., a retired candy manufacturer, established the John Birch society, a right-wing organization focused on exposing what it perceived to be the infiltration of communism into American society. At its peak, it claimed 100,000 members. It circulated its mission and influenced people through its widely distributed communications. This group called for the impeachment of Chief Justice Earl Warren following the Supreme Court's decisions in favor of civil liberties and desegregation.

At the 1983 Aryan Nations' World Congress, the White Power movement declared war on the United States. This meeting included speeches, a cross burning, and a swastika burning. It also featured a matchmaking dinner, leveraging the women in the group. Inclusion of women was often done to help normalize the activities and violent agenda of terrorist groups.

The Oath Keepers was incorporated in 2009 by founder Elmer Stewart Rhodes, a lawyer and former paratrooper. It is an American far-right antigovernment militia whose leaders have been convicted of violently opposing the government of the United States.

The Proud Boys was established by Gavin McInnes, co-founder of Vice Media, in 2016 during the U.S. presidential election. Proud Boys consider themselves "Western chauvinists." While they deny being racists, the organization is deeply rooted in White nationalism and misogyny.

On January 6, 2021, following the defeat of President Donald Trump in the 2020 U.S. presidential election, a mob attacked the United States Capitol Building in Washington, D.C. alleged to have been orchestrated by the Proud Boys and the Oath Keepers.

In 2021, the Southern Poverty Law Center in 2021 listed 50 "White nationalist" groups.[5] As of late, social media has been used to recruit and spread their ideology.

Women's Movement

The women's movement, typically referred to as the feminist movement, refers to a series of social and political campaigns calling for reforms on women's issues created by systemic inequities between men and women.

The Evolution of the Women's Movement

In the nineteenth and early twentieth centuries, a women's rights movement took place primarily focusing on legal rights. This included the right to vote, or women's suffrage. This was viewed as the first wave of feminism.

During this era, on October 16, 1916, Margaret Sanger opened the first birth control clinic in the United States. After her clinic in Brownsville, Brooklyn was declared illegal and raided, she closed the clinic and eventually founded the American Birth Control League in 1921—the precursor to Planned Parenthood.

In the 1960s and 70s, another women's rights movement took place. This is referred to as the second wave of feminism. The focus included politics, working rights, family, sexuality, etc. This second wave expanded to include women of varying socioeconomic statuses, women of color, and women from developing nations.

In the 1960s, women collaborated with government leaders and union representatives to lobby for equal pay and for protection against discrimination in employment. By the summer of 1966 the National Organization for Women (NOW) was established.

In the late 1960s, Gloria Steinem, an American journalist and social-political activist, emerged as a nationally recognized leader of second-wave of feminism in the United States. She was a co-founder of *Ms.* magazine.

In January 1973, in a landmark 7–2 decision in *Roe v. Wade*, the U.S. Supreme Court declared that the Constitution protects a woman's legal right to an abortion. In June 2022, the Supreme Court overturned the ruling.

Another wave of feminism took place in the mid-1990s and early 2010s. In the 1990s, Steinem helped establish "Take Our Daughters to Work Day."

During this period, several women ran and or were nominated for the first time for high-level political positions including the first woman to sit on the Supreme Court, Sandra

Day O'Connor, and the first speaker of the U.S. House of Representatives, Nancy Pelosi.

The "Me Too" movement was founded in 2006 by Tarana Burke to support survivors of sexual violence, particularly young women of color from underresourced communities.

The Lilly Ledbetter Fair Pay Act of 2009 was signed by President Barack Obama. It overturned The U.S. Supreme Court decision that limited the time period for filing compensation-related complaints of employment discrimination.

On January 21, 2017, the Women's March on Washington took place the day after the inauguration of Donald Trump as U.S. president. It was a worldwide protest to Trump's misogynistic rhetoric and policy positions, which were considered a threat to women's rights.

In Fall 2017, the #MeToo hashtag went viral and survivors across the globe came forward to share their experiences with sexual assault. This movement changed how many thought about sexual misconduct, gender, and power.

Inroads into the political sphere have continued in the 2010s and 2020s including the first woman to receive a nomination as a presidential candidate from a major political party, Hilary Clinton, and the first woman and woman of color to be sworn in as a vice president, Kamala Harris.

Economic Power

Looking at power in numbers through an economic lens, we have also seen groups leverage their consumer power to influence change in many of our institutions. Money talks!

Consumer Power and Marketing

The retail, restaurant, consumer goods, manufacturing, media, technology, professional services industries, and numerous others all rely on customers to stay in business. Market segmentation has been a stable practice to identify the nuanced needs of particular markets and develop products or variations of products that might appeal to a target market. The value and purchasing power of the Black, Hispanic, and Asian markets is astronomical and represents a huge opportunity for business brands and advertisers. The annual purchasing power ranges between $1.3 trillion and $1.8 trillion for each of these groups and is expected to continue to grow.

A 2018 Retail Customer Loyalty Study revealed that Black consumers are among the most loyal of all ethnic groups. The report indicated 48% of African Americans who find a good source for their purchases will tend to stick with it. This was compared to 35% of Americans overall.[6]

Globally, women control about $32 trillion in annual consumer spending. This was most recently demonstrated during summer 2023 at the box office where the movie *Barbie* reached the $1 billion mark. Additionally, the Beyoncé Renaissance tour and Taylor Swift Eras tour grossed millions, selling out in every city in which they were scheduled. The dominant audience for these concerts were women.

This purchasing power has the ability to influence corporations in terms of product design, advertising, and even workforce practices.

Additionally, there is an economic cost associated with racism. Former domestic policy advisor Susan Rice was met with mockery from social media in 2023 when she claimed that racism has cost the United States $16 trillion. She cited a report from Citibank, stating, "The analysis in the report shows that if four key racial gaps for Blacks—wages, education, housing, and investment—were closed 20 years ago, $16 trillion could have been added to the US economy. And if the gaps are closed today, $5 trillion can be added to US GDP over the next five years."[7]

Boycotts, Walkouts, and Strikes

The power of boycotts and strikes has been a long-standing way to use group power to influence change. Unions, along with grassroots organizations and small groups of citizens, have been able to give voice to social justice needs by bringing attention to inequitable practices and influencing and inspiring others to rally along.

There have been noted boycotts of retail outlets like Walmart and Chick-fil-A because of their policies or practices that adversely impact marginalized groups. During the writing of this book, several strikes were happening concurrently including the United Auto Workers, the Actors Guild, and the Writer's Guild. Collective bargaining is typically used as a measure to reconcile these disputes when unions are involved. Additionally, there are many social justice advocacy groups like Operation Push/Rainbow Coalition, which have challenged corporations on the public stage convincing them to create more equitable workplace practices.

Turning Back the Clock

In 2022 and 2023, major legislative changes occurred at the highest levels of our justice system, which would have one wonder if we have gone back to the future or entered the twilight zone! Examples include the dissolution of *Roe v. Wade* and the banning of affirmative action (specifically, race-conscious admissions) in higher education. Other movements organized by state and local jurisdictions and private citizens have also served to disrupt progress toward creating a more equitable society (e.g., redistricting or shutting down voting centers in communities of color, etc.). We have also seen the surge of several White supremacist groups and incidents that they have taken credit for or are alleged to have been involved in.

Such behaviors and movements can be simply defined as a confluence of fear, ego, and upsetting the apple cart. "Oh no, we have had a Black president, we can't let this happen again . . . and now the first woman vice president, also a woman of color. Whoa! Things are progressing too far . . ."

Lawsuits on Funding

As a case in point, a lawsuit against the Fearless Fund was filed before the Supreme Court by Edward Blum (of the American Alliance For Equal Rights). The Fearless Fund is an Atlanta-based firm that has invested nearly $27 million in about 40 businesses led by women of color, since launching in 2019. The Fund awarded another $3.7 million in grants. Collectively, those businesses employ about 540 individuals. The lawsuit indicates that this practice violates a section of the Civil Rights Act of 1964 prohibiting racial discrimination in contracts.

This investment capital provided by the Fearless Fund is a drop in the bucket of venture capital funding provided to small businesses. According to the nonprofit advocacy group digitalundivided, less than 1% of venture capital funding goes to businesses owned by Black and Hispanic women. Getting to 1% would take billions and it would take trillions to significantly move the needle.[8] Challenging these investment practices, as being illegal, serves to perpetuate the economic disparities experienced by marginalized groups.

Protests on Libraries

Did you ever in your wildest dreams think that while walking little Johnny or Stephanie to the library to check out a few books for the weekend that you would encounter a hostile crowd outside, demanding that it be shut down? Libraries have been viewed as a safe haven and free and accessible venues for completing school and work assignments and exploring the world through the insights and expertise of others. Yet, sadly, public libraries have become another target for far-right groups who are trying to reverse the progress made toward raising awareness, knowledge, and appreciation for the history of varying cultural groups within our society.

These far-right groups have attacked the principles of free speech and education by advocating for book bans and the discontinuance of library activities that provide education about marginalized groups like the LGBTQ+ community. There have been cases noted where the employees of these libraries have been threatened as well. This reflects a mindset that "if you don't see it, it doesn't or didn't exist." If we have no material about the Holocaust, then it becomes fictional. If we do not speak to the exploitation and suffering of groups like enslaved Africans and Asians confined to internment camps, then it didn't happen. If we do not allow our families to read about the presence of historically nontraditional family structures, then we prevent our citizens from viewing this as a possibility or seeing themselves reflected in the literature. Additionally, this censorship will elevate the frequency at which individuals rely on "fake news" and noncredible sources and key messages on social media. So to counter some of the disturbing narratives that are appearing, let me just say for the record, "Slavery Did Not Benefit Black People!"

The Threshold Effect

In Chapter 4, "Did You See Something? Bystanders and Allies," I spoke about the threshold that many organizations have in terms of the number of underrepresented groups entering their workforces. This is based on a culture of tokenism in which there is support for a few but not too many, especially as we look at senior leadership positions where strategic decisions are being made. I'm reminded of a TED Talk in which Mellody Hobson, co-CEO of Ariel Investments, speaks to an audience about being color blind versus color brave.[9] One example she gives is that if you were to walk into a room of senior leaders and see all Blacks or people of color sitting around the table, you would think that something was off there. However, if you were to the walk into a room full of all White males sitting around the table, you would think nothing of it. This tells me that there is a threshold for difference that we need to have courageous conversations about. This threshold effect is another way to maintain the status quo. It could be an unspoken or implicit norm within the culture, but it plays out in who is hired, promoted, and has a seat at the table.

The examples provided are just a few of many. They speak to different settings in which returning to or maintaining the status quo is pursued more diligently as dominant groups see the progression of historically marginalized groups. One might argue that this is human nature and we have seen this phenomenon across civilizations. It plays out in turf battles, takeovers, wars, colonization, genocide, regentrification, and other systemic practices. While we can't rewrite history (not that some aren't trying), we can learn from the harm our actions have created in the past and apply lessons learned in the settings in which we currently live and work.

Power in the Wrong Hands: How and Why We Reward Workplace Bullies

We scratch our heads wondering about individuals who we feel should be long gone from the workplace. "Why are they still here? Their behavior is outrageous and abusive! Their whole team is suffering from low morale."

There are several reasons why these workplace bullies are still around. One reason is that they have a close relationship with someone in charge, and this person is protecting them. This could be due to nepotism, or it could be based on a relationship from school or the old neighborhood.

Another reason is that this bully has a valued network outside of the organization. These stakeholders could be a book of clients, a group with political clout, or something related.

A very common reason is that this individual is extremely good at the technical aspects of their job, such as in bringing in new business or developing great business strategies and operations. But they may not be so good at leading and motivating the teams with whom they work. There are many who even have an abrasive management style and contribute to a hostile work environment. And yet these individuals remain key players within the organization and are often rewarded generously for their functional contribution, while their poor leadership skills are ignored.

Bullies come in all sizes, shapes, and colors. This behavior is not confined to any one gender, race, or sexual orientation. These individuals have been assigned legitimate power given the titles and roles they are in. They often have expert power as it relates to some technical area. But their lack of inclusive leadership skills and control-based behaviors can have damaging outcomes within the workplace.

Different Paradigms for Power

There have been many efforts at a systemic level to return the status of individuals back to the good old days. I believe that this can be explained by understanding that those who are in power do not want to lose it, and when they see other groups gaining on them in terms of power influence and visibility, this sparks fear. The mindset is "if you win, that means I lose." There is another way to look at these gains.

An Infinite Perspective on Power

In the book *Power: The Infinite Game* by Michael Broom and Donald Klein, the authors share that there is both a finite and infinite way to look at power within organizations. The infinite perspective on power understands that it is abundant and does not require struggle. Winning and losing are not at issue when playing infinitely. The purpose of infinite play is to sustain play rather than determine who wins and who loses. Applying this principle would suggest that there is collaboration, inclusion, and a balance in terms of when and how functional areas or individuals progress within their organizations, hence the notion of an infinite game. This can be contrasted with the finite organization which looks at power as a win-lose phenomena.

Several principles from this book resonate. Broom and Klein describe empowerment in the following way.

> *In an infinite organization, employees—managers and subordinates alike—are supported in believing in themselves and in one another. They are supported in stretching themselves, individually and collectively, so that they can identify and resolve their own conflicts and problems. In the process, they are likely to discover their inherent excellence while improving organizational functioning.*[10]

Cultural Paradigms of Power

We can also look at power through the lens of countries and culture. Both Hofstede's and Trompenaars frameworks address this.

Research conducted by Geert Hofstede has shown that there are cultural differences in terms of the degree to which members within a society accept or reject the unequal distribution of power within their societies. Members from countries with high levels of power-distance naturally follow a hierarchical order without questioning the justification for their places within their societies. This was found to be evident in certain countries, such as China and Japan. Accordingly, members within these countries value formality, respect, and hierarchy.[11]

In contrast, United States and Australia are countries with low levels of power-distance. They value a more egalitarian mindset, where hierarchies are challenged . . .

I'll let you absorb this for a second . . . the fact that America has low levels of power-distance only suggests that our citizens question the justification of hierarchy and the high levels of power assigned to individuals. But it doesn't mean these hierarchical structures don't exist. To our benefit we are at least questioning and challenging these structures.

If we revisit one of the dimensions in Trompenaars's Six Dimensions of Culture model, Achievement vs. Ascription, we can see how it relates to both power and privilege. These two aspects describe how a culture assesses a person's value. Achievement cultures gauge an individual's worth by their performance and actions, demanding constant validation. Conversely, Ascription cultures form judgments about a person based on attributes like gender or age, ascribing qualities to them merely because of their assigned role, or birthright.[12]

Empowerment

Thus far we have looked at ways that groups have empowered themselves to be a force for change, how those in power have responded, and different frameworks for understanding power. Let's look at how empowerment applies to individuals. I believe when we hear the word empowerment, we think of how a leader can empower their employees so that they are more functional and can reach their potential in the workplace. But empowerment is something that is owned by an individual or community. Saying that someone empowers someone else suggests that power can be given, held back, or taken away. This is actually disempowering.

When we are empowered, we have the ability to make purposeful choices that contribute to our aspirations and goals. We are able to express ourselves in authentic ways. We can transform our lives and the lives of those around us. So just how do we empower ourselves?

- **Growth mindset:** Empowerment is a lifelong process. You may feel empowered in one setting or for one season but not another.

I believe the key to sustainability is adopting a growth mindset, believing that you are capable of growing and changing when needed. This means that you believe your effort can lead to mastery, that failure is just a temporary setback, and that you can learn and benefit from feedback. This mindset helps us build resiliency, which is much needed because our lives are more like a marathon than a sprint.

- **Reading the culture**: There are many decision points that you will come across in the course of your career. You may feel that you have been at the receiving end of unfair practices. You may decide that you will bring this to the attention of those who can do something about it. This is when leveraging timing and political savvy are critical. If you have been with an organization long enough, hopefully you have learned about some of the unspoken rules of the culture, which might include who the true influencers are, or the protocol for sharing complaints, or seeking advice. Will it be a career-damaging effort if you skip your manager to talk to the VP of your department about a promotion? Will talking about inequities in compensation at a town hall meeting net you the desired results? The answer is "It depends." It depends on the norms of the culture. This is an area where it would benefit and empower you to know as much as you can. You can learn by observation, but you can also learn by testing some of your assumptions with others. Knowledge about the culture will enable you to implement a strategy that helps you reach your goals. Knowing how to read the culture and factoring that into your strategy is empowering.

- **Expert power**: Displaying expert power is a way to demonstrate empowerment. Once people recognize that you have credible expertise, you will become the go-to person for specific projects and assignments. You can become an influencer within your organization. You can leverage this visibility to build relationships and sponsorship to advance within your career. Expert power is a steppingstone to receiving legitimate power.

- **Follow your calling:** I recently viewed a videotape where Oprah Winfrey was interviewed. She spoke about careers versus a calling—that when we find our purpose in life it brings us inner fulfillment. When we are purpose driven and passionate about our work, we would pursue it even if we were not getting paid.[13] So, to the extent possible, I would encourage you to find a way to engage in things that you are passionate about. Now, all of this may not take place inside the workplace. Your passion may be connected to outside hobbies, activities, or community engagement. Spending time doing the things that matter most to you is empowering. You are indeed fortunate if you are able to demonstrate that passion within your career.

- **Self-care:** Self empowerment requires self-care. In relation to this I am reminded of the Black tax that many African American feel we have to pay in order to succeed in society. The Black tax refers to feeling the need to work harder and pay more to reach the same level of wealth, respect, and credibility as our White counterparts. Many of our parents instilled in us the need to work twice as hard to get half as far. When we step back and think of this, it is an exhausting way to lead one's life yet many of us are still doing so this way. This style of life may help you reach that brass ring but not without some cost to relationships, to your health, to your spirit. So, an empowering approach would be to prioritize your well-being and self-care, to take time for rest, and pursue activities and relationships that fulfill and restore you.

  Self-care may require reaching out to a professional. This might include a mental health professional. It might mean reaching out to a financial advisor or connecting with counselors within your religious institutions. Reaching out for help enables you to get out of your own head and leverage those who have experience with the challenges you may be facing. Reaching out for help, especially from a mental health professional, has been stigmatized in many communities including the Black community. I've seen this stigma fade as many community groups have advocated and changed the narrative around mental health so that it is viewed as a normal versus aberrant behavior. There is no health without mental health.

- **A higher power:** Another thing to remember is that when we constantly look for external validation, we put limitations on ourselves. Being a man of great faith, I believe that there is a higher power and this higher power can guide us through our lives and help us face all challenges. My faith has enabled me to be resilient, to survive setbacks, and to thrive and advance higher than my imagination could take me. However you refer to a higher power in your life—God, Allah, the Universe, or a voice from within—I would remind you to put your energy and trust in the hands of this power as you go through life's journey.

Using Our Power to Empower

What role do organizational leaders play in empowerment? Leaders can create environments that facilitate greater empowerment. Some suggestions and considerations include:

- Most organizations pride themselves on implementing consistent, standardized practices (equality), but this does not always have the same impact for different groups. Creating an environment that facilitates empowerment starts with understanding the different needs of individuals within your work team and appreciating that one size does not fit all (equity).
- Create assignments and networking opportunities that promote the growth of your team members.
- Be aware of how you use your own power and the impact it has on others.
- Empowering others can be as simple as giving them a voice, or helping them to see the big picture.

- Utilize allyship to advocate for your employees and promote a psychologically safe workplace that does not penalize individuals for challenging status quo or taking calculated risks.
- Address toxic behaviors that show up on your team and nip them in the bud.

A Closer Look at Privilege

If you haven't picked up on it yet, let me just share that my current role as a senior vice president requires me to constantly travel to the different cities and countries in which we have offices and hotels. Because of my frequent flyer status, I have earned VIP access, which enables me to do certain things that other passengers cannot. For me this is a privilege because I do not have to wait as long as others. I am escorted onto the plane, seated in first class. When others see me whizzing by, I am met with a number of reactions. Most people believe I am doing something I shouldn't be, that there's no way I should be getting on the plane ahead of them. I link this back to feelings of entitlement from those born into privilege. I would argue that I have earned privileges gained through my work, which requires extensive flying, but because of the color of my skin and the fact that I am not a well-known entertainer, athlete, or other celebrity, my actions are questioned.

A Picture Is Worth a Thousand Words

As one final personal example, I recall a flight where I was sitting in my seat in first class—1A. A man came onto the plane and apparently had a seat next to mine—1B. He looked at me in disbelief. He then called out to the flight attendant and proclaimed, "This man is in the wrong seat!" The flight attendant looked at the flight list and said to me, "Sir, I'm sorry but you're sitting in Mr. Stoudemire's seat." I looked at her and said, "What makes you think I'm not Mr. Stoudemire?" She and the passenger looked at me in a challenging way as though that was going to force me out of my seat. By this flight, I had grown so used to this behavior, so instead of going back and forth with them I simply pulled out my magazine, on which I was on the front cover, and left it alone. I could hear the flight attendant gasp and could tell that she was quite embarrassed as the magazine cover conveyed my executive status. At this point she apologized and tried to make amends. The man next to me however never did acknowledge or apologize for his rude behavior. Coupled with his sense of entitlement and privilege, his belief that I was where I didn't belong was stronger than the evidence in front of him.

Privilege is a first cousin to power. As stated, it is unearned access to resources only readily available to some people as a result of their advantaged social group membership. While this definition of privilege connects it to dominant groups, everyone is privileged in different ways. Our privilege can be connected to the context in which we operate.

If we take a minute to think about it, there are certain circumstances in which we all have privilege. For example, if you're going to a play or the theater and your seat is in the balcony, you probably think nothing of walking up the steps or down them to get to your reserved seats. However, I have witnessed a number of individuals who have come with wheelchair-bound family members and have had to miss part of the show because there was not a ramp or elevator that allowed them access to their seats.

For individuals who are right-handed, picking up a pair of scissors or even a golf club doesn't register a need to make adjustments in how you use them. But for our left-handed brothers and sisters this could provide a challenge.

As we discussed before, beauty and height are associated with other desirable qualities within our society and because of this bias we find these attributes playing a role in who gets hired, who gets promoted, who gets opportunities to be visible in front of clients.

Going to certain schools, even though you may have gained access because of your legacy status, enables you to be considered for jobs at premier consulting firms and corporations. Living in a community that receives adequate state and local resources enables you to drive to work without worrying about flattening your tire on potholes that have gone unrepaired for months or driving down a street where a road comes to an end. My view of privilege has expanded given my global travels. I know that based on being a U.S. citizen and having certain infrastructure main-tenance in place, there are many privileges that I enjoy that residents in other countries may not. This is adopting a glass-half-full versus a glass-half-empty mindset.

Notwithstanding, privilege does create disparities in the workplace and outside of it. In a 1989 article written by scholar, feminist, and anti-racist activist Peggy McIntosh, she speaks about White privilege. In this work, entitled "White Privilege: Unpacking the Invisible Knapsack," she states,

> I have come to see White privilege as an invisible package of unearned assets which I can count on cashing in each day, but about which I was "meant" to remain oblivious. White privilege is like an invisible weightless knapsack of special provisions, maps, passports, code-books, visas, clothes, tools and blank checks.[14]

McIntosh provides many of the benefits of White privilege such as:

- "I can do well in a challenging situation without being labeled a credit to my race."
- "I can be sure that my children will be given curricular activities and materials that testify to the existence of their race."

- "I can go shopping alone most of the time pretty well assured that I will not be followed or harassed."
- "I can go home from most meetings feeling somewhat tied in rather than isolated, out of place, outnumbered, unheard, held at a distance, or feared."

White privilege has been referenced extensively in research and literature. Other common types of privilege are those based on religion, gender, sexual orientation, and ableism. For example, with Christian privilege, one can expect to have time off work to celebrate religious holidays. With male privilege, the decision to hire him will never be based on assumptions about whether or not he might choose to have a family sometime soon. With heterosexual privilege, one can talk openly about their relationship, vacations, and family planning without worrying about being judged as immoral.

Training and discussions to raise awareness around privilege have helped change workplace policies and norms to some extent. This varies by industry and region of the country. For example, working in the Bible Belt states in the South one might expect Christian privilege to be predominant within organizations.

Revisiting "Karen"

To wrap things up, let's revisit one more personification of privilege. The reference to Karen has become synonymous with White women exploiting their privilege and power. This behavior was evident in a Central Park incident in 2020 in which a White woman, Amy Cooper, harassed a Black male who was bird watching in the park, after he asked her to control her dog. She, in fact, called the police to have this individual arrested. This videotaped encounter took on national acclaim and Cooper became known as "Central Park Karen." There have been several other "Karens" caught on video recordings. One example included a White woman who called the police on her Black neighbors for hosting a barbecue. These examples highlight how even historically marginalized groups, e.g., White women, can misuse privilege given the context.

Hearing stories like these, one might think, "Okay, these are a few individuals who just got it wrong." But let's take a deeper dive. Had the tables been turned with a Black woman calling the police on a White family or on a White man bird watching, what would the outcome have been? It is because of the unearned privilege that White women hold in society that enables them to initiate these activities. It is a sense of entitlement that directs these individuals to nip in the bud anything that makes them feel threatened or uncomfortable and to use their resources, that being law enforcement, to seal the deal. Additionally, this behavior may occur when no threat is felt, but as a way to assert one's status and keep someone else in their place.

Entitlement is the mindset that one is inherently deserving of special privileges. Now this could be due either to one's status or birthright or it could be someone having a "you owe me mentality." So, to be fair we can see how an entitlement mindset might show up in both dominant and marginalized groups.

In closing, the examples of power and privilege presented in this chapter are not meant to focus on blame. My intent is to raise awareness and provide some historical context for why power imbalances occur and how privilege and entitlement mindsets alongside it can contribute to inequities within society and the workplace. Understanding these issues is an essential first step for moving forward and implementing effective change solutions. Without this knowledge, any tactic or change strategy would be akin to putting on a pair of skates to go swimming.

I hope that you are encouraged by the examples of the positive use of power as well as reminded of the control you have over your own empowerment. The good news is that we don't have to wait for external conditions to be ideal before we can take action. Change begins with us!

In a world where you can be anything, Be kind.

—Jennifer Dukes Lee

Tactical Tools/Considerations

In the sections in this chapter, I have provided several considerations for self-empowerment and suggest ways that leaders can create environments that facilitate empowerment. I encourage you to revisit those sections, and I simply outline the points made earlier here.

Individuals can:

- Adopt a growth mindset.
- Learn to read the culture.
- Leverage expert power.
- Follow your calling.
- Employ self-care.
- Call on a Higher Power.

Organizational leaders and practitioners can:

- Develop an understanding of the different needs of individuals within your work team.
- Create growth opportunities.
- Be aware of how you use your own power.
- Find opportunities to give employees a voice.
- Utilize allyship.
- Nip toxic behaviors in the bud.

6

Stereotypes

The Help

I remember a time I went down to meet with one of my company's largest clients. They were located in Texas. We brought our entire team. We were all gathered in the conference room and the head of HR walks in and says "OK I'm ready to get started. Time is limited. Pour the coffee and pass these reports out."

She was talking to me. She assumed that I was the hired help. We sat down and I said, "I know you're busy and we want to get started. I'm Tyronne Stoudemire, the cluster manager for your account." She continued talking as if she hadn't heard me. She asked questions directly to one of my White team members, David (not his real name). David was so nervous. You could see it in his body language. He was working up a sweat. At one point he said, "You keep talking to me but I'm not in charge. He's in charge." He was pointing at me.

At this point she said, "Okay, let's take a break and come back." She got up and stepped away. Again, she couldn't believe I was the one there leading the team and providing her with the results. I walked over to her and said, "I understand that you didn't know who I was. I don't want this to stop us from moving forward. If you have a problem with my presence just let me know; we can try something different." I wanted to make sure that I confronted the issue but in a way that didn't totally disarm her. She made an attempt to reconcile and apologize during the break and, ultimately, we became friendly colleagues over time. But in this situation, I had to work twice as hard to position myself, as the White male who reported to me, based on the stereotype that she held about me.

I can think of numerous other incidents that I and my colleagues have been in where we have been mistaken for assistants, retail clerks, anything but leaders. These assumptions are based on stereotypes that peg people of color into helping roles and White males into leadership roles—even in the face of hard evidence.

Not all birds can fly.

Spell It out for Me

A stereotype is an overgeneralization about an individual based on a group that they belong to. Stereotypes can apply to any group, whether they be within the majority or minority. They can apply to cultural groups, professional groups, certain regions, or to a particular industry. Stereotypes are also applicable when we think of different generational and religious groups. Stereotypes can be positive and negative, but they are often misconceptions or misrepresentations.

We can better understand the concept of stereotype when comparing it to an archetype. An archetype is the tendency of a group of people who share a common background to behave in a certain way. Often research based on statistical or historical patterns support these archetypes. In contrast a stereotype is the belief that all members who belong to a particular group will have the same traits or behave in the same way. It is an oversimplified mental picture that one has and is often based on limited information.

Stereotypes often lead to prejudice—prejudging others without sufficient evidence. This can lead to negative feelings, bias, discrimination, and neglect. All of these resulting outcomes can have adverse impacts on specific groups, particularly in the workplace.

Stereotypes are prevalent. I don't believe any of us are exempt from this thinking. We all make assumptions about individuals, and there are several reasons why we do so. Just like the assumptions that were made about me and my team in my client's conference room, I've made assumptions about others. My point is that while we may all have stereotypes, we need to reflect and pause before we act on them. Similar to bias, this requires self-awareness and reflection to understand who and why we stereotype and from where our stereotypes originated.

How Do Stereotypes Evolve?

Have you ever gripped your purse a little tighter or checked your back pocket upon entering an elevator occupied by a Latino or Black teenager? Do you avoid going into a club or restaurant if you hear country western music playing and see a group of bikers standing outside?

A stereotype is an impression that we have formed; but these impressions are largely due to how we have been socialized. They come from our personal experiences with our family, with our friends and communities. We often learn different rules and expectations about who is able to do what, who has status and who doesn't, what is attractive and what isn't, what is weak and what is strong, what is dangerous and what is safe. Hearing or overhearing these conversations on a repeated basis imprints them into our unconscious minds. We often don't even recall how these stereotypes were formed, but similar to our implicit biases we tend to look at the world through these stereotypical lenses.

Little Miss Muffet sat on a tuffet, eating her curds and whey . . .

Along came a spider who sat down beside her and scared Little Miss Muffet away[1]

For example, gender stereotypes have been prevalent in the literature for centuries. I'm sure you can remember having read or having an adult in your life read to you a fairy tale or nursery rhyme to help you go to sleep at night. Many of our classic childrens' books and fairy tales often depict women as being helpless, needing to be rescued, and, conversely, depict men as the heroes. These types of stories and illustrations reinforce gender roles that no longer apply. There has been research that shows that children start to develop beliefs about gender at the age of two. This includes stereotypes like boys are stronger or better at math and that girls are more nurturing and are better at reading.

Fairy tales also often depict villains as being individuals from foreign cultures or from a marginalized group. The majority of heroes and heroines are White. For centuries Whites have controlled the broader American culture and in doing so have perpetuated European-based folklore to the exclusion of the folklores of African, Asian, Hispanic, Middle Eastern, and other cultures. The stories of people of color have been omitted or misrepresented; and these same individuals have been prohibited from participating in the stories that are allowed. These depictions and omissions have been challenged lately in the remake of animated films by placing people of color in the main roles. You may be familiar with all the outcry that followed after announcing that *The Little Mermaid* (2023) character Ariel would be played by Halle Bailey, a young Black woman.

Stereotypes are present in the early educational experience of our youth as well. One example would include how children are guided or not guided into certain professions. There have been numerous publicized examples of school guidance counselors suggesting that only certain professions were relevant for women, for Blacks and Hispanics. Women were often guided into helping and nurturing professions like teaching and nursing versus being encouraged to pursue a medical degree and become physicians. Students of color and women were often discouraged from going into the STEM (Science, Technology, Engineering, Math) areas. Black male youth are stigmatized as early as third grade as being overly aggressive underachievers requiring discipline, which results in them being ostracized and isolated. This contributes to more extreme disciplinary practices as well as to the school-to-prison pipeline.

Thank goodness for the many community groups that are supplementing the academic experience of our youth and exposing them to career paths, mentors, and individuals who can help dispel the stereotypes they have learned or been subjected to. For example, I recall Mae Jemison, a Black female astronaut raised in Chicago, making her rounds at different schools and strongly encouraging students of color and women to consider going into the aeronautical professions. Representation matters!

Representation is the Manifestation of our Dreams!

Given our social environment shapes the way we see the world, we can understand that if we have a social network in which everybody looks like us, walks like us, and talks like us, then we have limited data on other groups. A study conducted in 2016 by Cox and colleagues found that when looking at the homogeneity of the social network, 75% of White Americans reported that their network was only comprised of other White people. This same finding can be generalized, to large extent, to any other groups who do not engage with individuals from different backgrounds.[2] Perceptions that they have will be restricted to what they have heard and what has been reinforced in the systems in which they are a part.

The Evolution and Perpetuation of Stereotypes Through Mass Media

Stereotypes were frequently used for comedic purposes and to justify discriminatory practices. For example, early-eighteenth-century practices presented African Americans in inhumane manners, as ignorant, clownish, and animalistic. African Americans were not even afforded the opportunity to play themselves. Instead, Whites dressed in black-face to mock African Americans and reinforce White supremacy. During this period, there were numerous protests against stereotypical and demeaning characterizations; yet the industry continued perpetuating these narratives and provided limited opportunities for minorities to participate.

In the nineteenth and early twentieth centuries, media such as newspapers, cartoons, and theater played a significant role in perpetuating racial and ethnic stereotypes. For example, African Americans were often depicted as caricatures or "minstrels," reinforcing derogatory stereotypes. One of the most egregious films that served as a catalyst for African Americans to produce their own films was *The Birth of a Nation* in 1915, which glorified the Ku Klux Klan and depicted Blacks as inferior beings.[3]

The advent of television brought new opportunities for both challenging and perpetuating stereotypes. Shows like *I Love Lucy* broke ground by featuring interracial marriages and a strong female lead, although still relegated to a role where most women weren't provided the option of having careers. Yet, many other shows continued to rely on stereotypes for humor and storytelling. Blacks were often portrayed in subservient roles or as criminals.

Television and film also exploited the Jewish mother stereotype, which generally involved a loud, highly talkative, overprotective, and overbearing mother, interfering in her adult children's lives and bringing up things to make them feel guilty. The Jewish-American princess (JAP) or spoiled brat depiction also became prevalent along with the miserly Jewish father.

Latinos have been overrepresented in roles as maids, gardeners, pool boys, or gang members. The women are often oversexualized or staunch Catholics—picture the *abuela* praying with a rosary clad tightly in her hands. Irish Americans are often depicted as drunks, while Italian Americans are often associated with the mafia. The LGBTQ+ and differently abled communities largely have been treated as if they don't exist, and when they are represented, their personas are often stereotypical exaggerations.

Comedians regularly base their sketches on stereotypes; and tend to poke fun at groups to which they belong. This is generally received with roaring laughter and applause from their audiences. While it is understood that this type of humor is expected, it still feeds into already believed stereotypes. Some might argue that comedy presents a teachable moment because it exaggerates stereotypes and points to the ridiculousness of them. Nevertheless, what happens on stage has no space in the workplace.

The proliferation of cable, streaming services, the internet, and social media has diversified the media landscape. This has amplified more diverse narratives as well as contributed to the spread of stereotypes. Individuals and groups have leveraged these media to call out the film and other media industries for their lack of positive representation of marginalized groups. The real-time communication inherent in platforms like X (formerly Twitter), TikTok, and Instagram allows for real-time recording and reporting.

Historically, commercials and advertisements for cleaning products often depicted women as the primary users. Men were rarely shown in such roles, reinforcing the stereotype that cleaning is a woman's job. Toy advertisements have traditionally promoted gender-specific toys, with boys being encouraged to play with action figures, cars, and building sets, while girls were marketed dolls, kitchen sets, and makeup kits. This reinforced the idea that certain toys are suitable for one gender but not the other.

Advertisements for fashion and beauty products often featured unrealistic and idealized portrayals of women and men, promoting a narrow definition of desirable femininity or masculinity. Automobile commercials frequently portrayed men as the primary target audience, emphasizing power, speed, and status while women were often just passively sitting along for the ride.

I have noticed significant changes in this realm within the last decade. Commercials and ads, now, seem to proliferate with interracial couples, same-sex couples, full-figured models and actors, and more marketing of cosmetic products and procedures to men.

A Tale of Two First Ladies

In the workplace, African American women are faced with preconceptions and expectations that have been dictated by history. Looking back just a few generations, African American women roles in the workplace often have been those that are subservient to others. She has been the maid, nanny, caretaker, or the one performing menial or entry-level jobs. These roles have been associated with stereotypes, such as the mammy, the jezebel, and the sapphire. These known stereotypes for African American women have a historical past, stemming from the Jim Crow era. The mammy is considered the loyal, desexualized, self-sacrificing nurturer. The jezebel is viewed as overtly sexualized and assertive. Lastly, the sapphire is seen as assertive, comical, emasculating, and obsessed with status climbing.

Another stereotype assigned to African American women is the concept of the "Angry Black Woman." She is viewed as emotional, irrational, hostile, and negative. Whenever she expresses an opposing view, images of her raising her eyebrows, twisting her neck and being angry for the sake of being angry are conjured. The power of this stereotype results in African American women often suppressing their feelings.

The former First Lady of the United States, Michelle Obama, had to actively work at dispelling this myth as it was often applied to her within the media. In an article by Durr and Wingfield (2011), it was pointed out how two of America's former first ladies, Michelle Obama and Hillary Clinton, were similar in how they addressed the world. They each were intelligent and accomplished, however they were described differently due to their race. Hillary Clinton was viewed as an overbearing, emasculating feminist. Alternatively, Michelle Obama had to contend with the gendered racial stereotype of the Angry Black Woman stemming from the sapphire stereotype, which describes Black women as domineering, loud, and blunt.[4]

Michelle Obama overcame this misconception. She was able to transcend this stereotype given her global platform, unquestionable professionalism, and community-centered narrative. She has inspired a nation of young women by being a visible role model.

Who Do Stereotypes Benefit?

Stereotypes are often perpetuated to justify the discrimination and unequal treatment of specific groups while reinforcing the privilege of others. They are generally created and communicated by dominant groups that have the power and capacity to shape policy, legislation, communication, and other systemic practices. This does not mean that they are not perpetuated by marginalized groups. For example, a group of Black or Latina Christian women may hold certain stereotypes about members in the LGBTQ+ community or about White Republicans.

Not all stereotypes are negative ones. For example, the academic success of Asian Americans and their proficiency in math has been a stereotype. This could be viewed positively. Yet, it is still a misconception. While it might be based on statistical trends that Asian Americans perform better in these areas overall compared to other groups, this would make it an archetype. It would become a stereotype once we jump to the conclusion that every person who is Asian American is going to be good at math.

Anytime we rely on stereotypes we reduce an individual to a limited and often inaccurate persona. So, for example, assuming Asian Americans are good in math and technology areas often leads to guidance counselors and employers neglecting to encourage them to pursue other areas such as leadership positions. As another example, applying the stereotype that all Jewish Americans are wealthy or are good lawyers is also a misconception. Similarly, not all Blacks have athletic ability and can dance; and not all women are nurturing.

Guilty by Association

On another of the many flights I've been on, there was a man who boarded who was from India. At one point during the flight he got up to go into the bathroom, right after another man (who happened to be White) came out. Apparently, the White guy had left the bathroom a bona fide mess. The Indian guy came out and chastised the White guy. They got into a back and forth confrontation. "You're nasty!" "Get out of my face." This went on and on, and I knew I didn't want to be involved in any part of the drama.

Eventually the plane landed and when the door was opened the police come in to arrest the Indian guy and me! They assumed I knew him and was in cahoots with him. He wasn't even sitting next to me! He was sitting somewhere behind me. But they accosted both of us, took us off of the plane and detained us in this tiny back room.

I kept telling them I did not know this person; I was not with him. The flight attendant who had been on with us even vouched for me at some point, saying she didn't think I was with him, either. But they made the assumption that I was involved because we were two people of color sitting in the same area! I guess they assumed I was from India as well, and I have often been mistaken for Indian because of my skin tone and hair texture.

It was a scary situation. I didn't want to go to jail because of two people fighting about the toilet! I didn't open my mouth, though. I just let them check things out. After they investigated the list of people who were on the plane, they were able to tell that we weren't together and eventually let me go. But prior to that, I was guilty by (their) association, and I wasn't even associated!

Overlooked Evidence

We tend to rely on stereotypes when other information is missing so, for example, if we know nothing about an individual except for the group that they are part of, or if we know a little bit about the person but not much, we tend to fill in the blanks with what we have heard or what we infer.

This reminds me of a model that I have used in my work called the "ladder of inference."[5,6] Picture this. You are in a situation where you observe some visible data about an individual. For example, I'm sitting in the same section of the plane as an individual who is wearing a Topi. You jump to the top of the ladder with your conclusion that I am associated with this person because we have a similar complexion and look like we might be from the same country. This is an inference that has been made without looking for more data. We jump to faulty conclusions or skip rungs on the ladder when we should be collecting more data and observing more before taking action, but we often do not. I'll refer back to my flight experience to highlight how the officers quickly climbed the ladder of inference when they detained me. But in the face of evidence, or lack of it, they had to slowly climb back down, consider the evidence that they overlooked, and take a different action, which to my benefit allowed me to go on my merry way.

Another model that is applicable here and widely used by practitioners is the D.I.N. framework—Describe, Interpret, Navigate (see Figure 6.1).

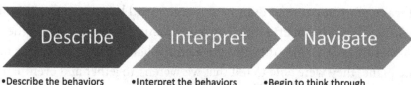

FIGURE 6.1 Describe, interpret, navigate (D.I.N.) model.

This is an offshoot of the D.I.E model, which is Describe, Interpret, Evaluate. Both models challenge us to be deliberate in our thinking and actions when we encounter new situations that involve cultural difference. They are usually leveraged in presentations or training activities to help people describe, without judgment, what they see and then begin to interpret it through their lens as well as to think about what it might mean through someone else's worldview. These steps are critical prior to conclusions being made or actions being taken. Thinking through what you've seen versus how you have interpreted it enables you to think of relevant solutions for navigating and responding appropriately.

Because of the stereotyping and assumptions that were made in the flight situation mentioned, I was deemed to be guilty by association. This is generally an emotional reaction versus one based on logic or observation. It is a shortcut that people use, either subconsciously or consciously, to justify their actions. The ladder of inference and D.I.N. frameworks give us an option to avoid these mental shortcuts.

The Impact of Stereotypes

Harboring and acting on stereotypes can lead to prejudice, discrimination, and other behaviors that limit inclusion and belonging. At a societal level, stereotypes reinforce systemic and structural inequities that result in disparities in education, healthcare, income, criminal justice, etc. These outcomes are significant. In the workplace, there are several negative impacts that stereotypes can contribute to.

Pay Inequities

Women and employees of color are often underutilized and underpaid compared to their White male counterparts, in large part because of assumptions made about their commitment to work and their skill and competency.

Looking at work-life balance, stereotypes about women prioritizing family over career or men being more career focused can lead to inequitable treatment of both of these groups. It can result in inequities related to the application of parental leave policies or allowing for flexible work arrangements.

Stereotypes and Leadership

When we look at career opportunities, there are assumptions made about the attributes needed to be successful in certain roles. Those attributes that are aligned with leadership roles have generally been aligned with characteristics considered to be male, traits like being more assertive or ambitious. Consequently, this plays out in who is considered and who advances into leadership. White males have been viewed as being more naturally suited for leadership positions. Women and groups like Asian Americans find it more challenging to break into these leadership roles.

Within organizations this has been addressed in a couple of ways. One is in recognizing the stereotype and understanding that the traits needed for leadership can manifest in any particular demographic group. The other way is to redefine what is necessary for leadership. Organizations have begun to look at the benefits of a more nurturing and people-development style of leadership. The characteristics of effective leaders can incorporate both masculine and feminine qualities depicting leadership more androgynously.

I have made it my mission to highlight opportunities to redefine stereotypical profiles of leadership wherever I can. One *Harvard Business Review* article that addresses this, "It's Time to Rethink the Good Leader," highlights the dearth of Asian Americans in leadership. This article cites several research findings that are listed in the "Stereotypes and Asian Americans in the Workplace" sidebar.

Stereotypes and Asian Americans in the Workplace

- Since the 1960s, Asian Americans have become the country's "model minority," largely due to significant increases in economic mobility that have mostly been attributed to education.
- Stereotypes about Asians being highly competent can make Asians appear threatening in the workplace, and stereotypes about Asians lacking social skills make them seem unfit for leadership.
- Within the big tech firms, Asian Americans (including Indians) are 27% of the workers in these companies, but only 19% of managers and 14% of executives (and only 3.1% for Asian women). This underrepresentation in leadership is referred to as the "bamboo ceiling." In contrast, Whites represented 62% of professionals and 80% of executives in these firms.
- Whites are threatened by the "unfairly high" levels of competence possessed by Asians and essentially use the

stereotype that Asians lack social skill as a pretext for discrimination.

- Individuals who held stereotypical views of Asians were less likely to want to interact with or learn more about Asians. For example, both high-competence and low-sociability ratings of Asians were negatively correlated with individuals wanting to be roommates with an Asian person.
- Asians face a double bind. If they act more dominant, they will be less liked, but if they do not project dominance, they will not be seen as leaders.
- Evidence shows that neither men nor women prefer to be treated in an aggressive fashion, yet that model persists as a valid expectation for leadership.
- Bottom line: businesses should focus on determining the competencies needed to fulfill a leadership job and then select leaders who fit the requirements rather than leadership stereotypes.[7]

Whether it is the bamboo, glass, or concrete ceiling (a term that reflects the often inpenetrable advancement barrier for women of color), employees who face constant criticism or don't get well-deserved promotions because of stereotyping can lose motivation and interest in performing their jobs. This often leads to decreased morale and productivity, and employee turnover.

The stress that results from experiencing stereotype-driven behaviors and discrimination can have adverse effects on an individual's mental and physical health. When you are exposed to and aware of the stereotypes associated with your group, this can lead to you internalizing the negative aspects of that stereotype, leading to self-fulfilling prophecies of that stereotype.

Stereotype Threat

Being aware of negative stereotypes leads to anxiety and decreased performance—a phenomenon known as *stereotype threat*. This occurs when someone is always in fear of doing something that could potentially confirm a negative stereotype about them. This impacts both self-esteem and performance. There has been a lot of research done on this. In the United States, the term "racial battle fatigue" was introduced by William A. Smith (2003) to describe the physical and psychological stress responses experienced by people of color in predominantly White institutions (PWIs) of higher education, due to consistent experiences of discrimination, microaggressions, and stereotype threat.[8] This research started with Black men and Black women faculty members as well as college students and has expanded and become a critical framework for understanding the experiences of people of color in PWIs.

In a research article by Owens and colleagues, the authors point out the negative impact of stereotypes on performance as reported across multiple studies. It was found that the awareness of a negative stereotype that Black and Latino students were less intelligent than White and Asian students actually impacted their performance levels. In another study, Black and White students were given the same test. When the task was described as a test of ability, the students of color scored lower. However, when the test was described as a game, both Black and White students performed equally well. In another similar study, Black students were separated into two groups and given a test. One group was asked to write their name and ethnicity on the top of the page, while the other group wasn't. Those who wrote their ethnicity on the page did not perform as well as the other group. Similar results have been found in studies with women who were asked to identify their sex on the math tests that they took, and with more elderly individuals who were asked to identify their age on memory tests.[9] While these are examples that align with specific testing situations, the findings suggest that cues from our environment that trigger us to focus in on potentially negative aspects of ourselves make a difference in how effective or successful we can be.

Given this happens so often I have learned to turn an environmental trigger into an Ah Ha moment.

Take My Keys, Please!

I remember going to Orlando for a global leadership meeting. A group of us were standing outside of our hotel and about to go in. We were just casually talking. In the midst of this, a White guy pulls up in his Ferrari jumps out of his car, looks at the group, and throws his keys at me. So, what did I do? I got in his car and while he was still there I said, " I can't drive a stick. I'm not sure how to get this started." He responds, "What do you mean? Aren't you the valet? Don't you know how to drive every kind of car?" I responded, "No, I'm not the valet, but you gave me your keys. I've got witnesses, so I assumed you wanted me to take your car."

I bet he'll think twice before he does that again! As mentioned, I've learned how to make these incidents teachable moments while also having a little bit of fun with them.

Methods for Dismantling Stereotypes

I don't know that we will ever totally dismantle stereotypes, but I believe we can disrupt and create more awareness around them. Until the majority of us are willing to explore life outside of our cozy little cocoons we will tend to respond to others based on the slanted messages and images we received growing up, that are reinforced 24/7 through the media.

It is possible that every once in a while, we might engage with a Black woman who actually likes to swim or a Japanese American man who deplores math; but we will probably dismiss this as an exception to the rule. My hope is that we will become more intentional about connecting with individuals in order to build greater understanding, empathy and realistic images of the multifaceted nature of those around us.

Not everything that is faced can be changed; but nothing can be changed until it is faced.

—*James Baldwin*

Tactical Tools/Considerations

In this chapter, I have discussed stereotypes, how they came to be, and why they are so prevalent. Now look at things you can do to be aware of and dismantle stereotypes.
Individuals can:

- Think about how you might be climbing the ladder of inference before making instant judgments about others. Look for more data.
- Look for things that you have in common when you meet others as well as seek insight into their experiences that may be different. This helps build appreciation.
- Engage in educational activities to learn more about different cultures and groups. This would include reading, viewing films/videos, and listening to different news sources.
- Join groups to broaden your networks to include many individuals from diverse backgrounds, not just one or two individuals.
- Participate in an Employee Resource Group that represents a culture different from your own.

Organizational leaders and practitioners can:

- Increase representation and exposure to role models. It is important that others see individuals who are debunking the myths and stereotypes in senior and/or mission-critical roles. Seeing women and Asian American employees in senior leadership positions, for example, points to the power of representation. Hosting a guest speaker series where individuals come in and speak about how they have entered into nontraditional roles can be inspiring, especially for employees challenged with stereotype threat.
- Ensure there are explicit policies outlining codes of conduct for employees. This will help to create an environment where respect is demonstrated. Respect is a precursor to appreciation and can minimize the tendency to act based on stereotypes.
- Select a movie that may have controversial depictions of specific demographic groups, and invite a facilitator in to help small groups of employees debrief and discuss.
- Sponsor forums that bring different groups together and require them to collaborate outside of their structured roles. This could include creating volunteer teams for community efforts like Habitat for Humanity or Walk out of Darkness.
- Provide resources on your company's intranet. This could include a link to podcasts, videos, and articles that address stereotypes and debunk myths about specific cultural groups.
- Confront stereotypes. Similar to microinequities, if you hear someone making statements that are stereotypical, determine how you can make it a teachable moment. You could do so by drawing attention to the comment that was made

and asking questions that might get to why the person either believes what they are saying or whether there was some other intention.

- Leverage training carefully and strategically. There has been an ongoing debate of whether to focus on the topic of stereotypes in DEI training. This training has been viewed as contributing to stereotypes by acknowledging, validating, and perpetuating them. However, it is difficult to understand the impacts of a phenomenon if you don't discuss it. Stereotypes are inextricably aligned with implicit bias. The potential for positive outcomes are greater when training is accompanied by other initiatives that focus on awareness and skill building and are continued over a significant time period.

7

Be Like Us: Adapting to Organizational Culture

The Dominance of Organizational Culture

There is a commonly used adage in business that "culture eats strategy for lunch." It speaks to the fact that an organization can put together vision statements and strategies with detailed action plans and accountability, but if these actions bump up against the culture, they are doomed to be short-lived. The overarching culture of an organization can either enhance or deter efforts to create diverse, inclusive, and equitable environments.

We can all think of examples of organizations that have strong cultures. When I was growing up, I often heard references to the strong cultures of enterprises like IBM, Ford, General Electric, and Motown. The military has a strong dominant culture. Healthcare organizations often have very dominant cultures. These examples remind us that a dominant culture will be reflected in different ways. Today we have many of the tech giants like Google and Microsoft mentioned for their strong and influential cultures. You can walk into a Google or Zappos office and see that it personifies informality and creativity. Contrast that with walking inside Goldman Sachs or other financial institution on Wall Street and you will clearly note a difference. The walls breathe hierarchy, structure, and formality. You can see culture in action. The culture differences may or may not have a different impact on creating a sense of inclusion and belonging; but understanding the prevailing culture is a critical place to start.

Strong cultures have been shown to benefit companies. Research has shown that well-managed cultures deliver better financial results, including sales growth, profits, increased value to shareholders, and return on assets. Many of these organizations have a culture that clearly displays their values to the general public. For example, Toms has a very socially focused mission and demonstrates this by giving away one pair of shoes for every pair it sells. Conversely, there are some organizations that have been known for their unethical cultures. Think back to the scandals associated with Enron and Tyco.

What Is Culture?

Often when I am engaged with others in discussing organizational culture individuals immediately will think that I am speaking to the different cultural groups that make up the workforce's composition. This is only one aspect. Organizational culture is the overarching and inherent norms, values, and belief systems that influence the organization's policies, practices, and behaviors. This definition is similar to how culture would be defined for a specific societal group, which is often depicted as a shared system of beliefs, values, and behaviors that a group uses to survive and thrive. If we connect this back to an organizational culture, we can see many similarities. An organization, along with its operations, products, and services, leverages both spoken and unspoken codes to define what is valued, allowed, taboo, or sacred. Organizations use these codes to survive, stay competitive, and maintain control of how individuals interact with one another.

Edgar Shein, the most widely known theorist surrounding organizational culture described culture as:

> *A pattern of shared basic assumptions that was learned by a group as it solved its problems of external adaptation and internal integration, that has worked well enough to be considered valid and, therefore, to be taught to new members as the correct way to perceive, think, and feel in relation to those problems.*[1]

This is reflected in Shein's Elements of Culture (see Figure 7.1).

These shared values and beliefs guide employees on how to behave. Having a strong organizational culture means that the vision and values

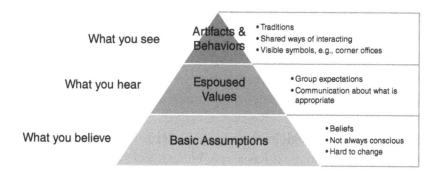

FIGURE 7.1 Schein's Elements of Culture.

are clear and well-defined. There is generally alignment between the espoused or spoken cultural expectations and the actual practices and behaviors. In other words, "What you see is what you get!"

For example, how we communicate with management is one aspect of culture. I remember working for one organization that espoused an egalitarian culture and indicated that management had an open-door policy, which meant you could pop your head into a senior leader's office with a question versus waiting weeks to get on their schedule. In other organizations in which I have worked, this was unheard of. You would never think it was appropriate to be walking down the hallway on the executive floor level. There were special elevators to get to this floor and you had better have had an invite and possibly an escort to be there!

Importance to DEI

A culture of inclusion is foundational to attracting and retaining competitive, diverse talent. Many organizations have figured out how to brand themselves and attract diverse talent into their organizations, but they are not always able to keep this talent. This revolving door is, in part, due to the dominant culture within the organization—a culture that views employees of color as a risk, or women as those who won't take their careers seriously. It is highly protective of the status quo and views confrontation or conflict as a negative.

Let's look at a hypothetical organization so that we can further discuss the implications of organizational culture on DEI efforts.

Organization XYZ is a global financial services firm, and the clients are Fortune 500 companies. It has a very hierarchical structure. There are many layers of management. The dress style is very conservative. In fact, there is a dress code that indicates what type of shirts, dresses, and shoes can be worn by employees. While there have been no references to other aspects of appearance, no man at the management level has any facial hair and their hair is cut very short. You do not see anyone with any tattoos, and in fact no one can remember the last time they saw anyone's arms exposed.

While this company has recently taken on a hybrid work format, the expectation is that individuals are in the office three to four days out of the week. Salaried employees work regularly into the evening based on client demands. Communication is shared on an as-needed basis and usually from the top down. If an employee has an issue, they either discuss it with their manager or go to HR. Sharing issues or ideas with a manager at any higher level is considered taboo. Confronting or criticizing management in an open forum (such as a town hall) is also condemned.

Holidays celebrated include New Year's, Good Friday, Memorial Day, Fourth of July, Labor Day, Thanksgiving, and Christmas. The organization provides floating holidays for individuals to take off for other observances. The annual Holiday party is celebrated the week before Christmas. It is considered tradition, and everyone is expected to attend and bring their spouses. The cafeteria, however, prepares appetizers and refreshments that represent different country cultures.

Within its communications on its website, this employer indicates it values its customers first; it values integrity and innovation. There are two Employee Resource Groups—one for Women and one for African Americans.

XYZ company has recently tried to expand into the Latin American market. They have opened up offices in this region as well as increased their recruiting efforts of Latinx candidates within the United States.

Does this sound like an organization you would want to work for? On the surface this may not sound like there would be a conflict for some, but let's create a hypothetical character Alejandro, an employee with XYZ.

XYZ recently hired Alejandro in a middle management role to manage one of their large call centers. During the interview process, the hiring manager and Alejandro's future coworkers indicated they were very impressed with his background and felt that he could be an asset to their organization. They indicated that he could be a good liaison between the United States and the offices they were trying to establish in Latin America. They mentioned that there were several DEI efforts in place. They encouraged Alejandro to bring his unique insights and give them feedback on where they could improve.

During Alejandro's first week, things seemed to be going okay. He went through orientation and onboarding and was introduced to several directors and VPs within the organization. He felt he had a good grasp of the current clients and expansion efforts.

After the third week, a few of the senior managers approached Alejandro and asked, "Do you mind if we call you Alex?" This concerned Alejandro, but he said he was fine with it given they kept butchering his name every time they said it. Almost within the same breath his manager said, "Alex, remember the company picnic is next weekend and we look forward to you and your family being there." Alejandro's niece's Quinceanera was that weekend and he mentioned this to his manager. His manager said why don't you bring her to the picnic, and we can celebrate that, and then you can leave a bit early to continue celebrating with your wife and family. Alejandro considered mentioning that he was not married and was actually living with his male partner. Instead, he decided not to mention this and simply call in sick the day before the picnic.

I could go on and on here, but I think this is enough information to see that Alejandro's authentic identity did not necessarily mesh with the dominating culture. His managers were not curious enough to learn more about Alejandro and made certain assumptions. They also discouraged him from challenging traditions even though the timeframe for celebration would have had significant implications for Alejandro. The expectation of assimilation was also evident in their request to substitute Alex for his real name. And while there are Employee Resource Groups in place, there do not appear to be any that support the LGBTQ+ community or Latinx employees.

It would be no surprise if Alejandro decided to leave this organization and exit through the revolving door. If he continued to work for XYZ, we could anticipate that he would feel disengaged and somewhat alienated given the dominating culture of the organization. This would most likely seep into his ability to motivate others and excel in his role.

This example highlights an organization that is most likely in the early phases of implementing DEI efforts. The focus may be on increasing diversity, leveraging employees for market purposes, and having some surface level support in place. But it does not appear that management has taken a close look at its organizational culture as reflected in its norms, communication preferences, traditions, and related practices.

Types of Organizational Cultures

How would you describe the organizational culture of XYZ company? There are probably many words that come to mind. Some of the more generic ways in which company or industry cultures have been labeled include one or more of the following:

Bureaucratic	Egalitarian	Innovative	Weak
Patriarchal	Informal	Inclusive	Risk averse
Formal	Playful	Family-oriented	Cutthroat
Traditional	Entrepreneurial	High-integrity	Competitive
Conservative	High-energy	Values difference	Up or out
Nonconfrontational	Creative	Culture of accountability	Sink or swim
Stuffy	Purpose driven		Culture of optionality
Passive-aggressive		Strong	

These labels, often used to define culture, speak to the overall persona of the organization. Some aspects may be more visible than others. They align with both the assumptions and espoused values in Schein's Elements of Culture model. For example, one might hear that an assumption or value of an organization is egalitarianism. At the artifact level, this might be displayed in the fact that everyone works in a cubicle or open space, and that leaders do not necessarily have corner offices.

Microcultures

Organizations like IBM, McKinsey, and Google are known for having strong cultures that are pervasive throughout their organizations, but it is very common for several minicultures to coexist within organizations. These subcultures are often linked to specific functional areas, business units, or geographic regions. Consequently, it is foreseeable that the espoused or spoken culture could be consistent throughout the organization, but that the way that culture is interpreted and manifested differs in different parts of the organization. For example, the client-facing departments of an organization may be more formal, competitive, and possibly even cutthroat. The financial department may be more risk averse. Technology departments might be more informal; the culture within the communications and public relations departments might be viewed as more creative.

How Conformance to Culture Is Achieved

Cultures generally evolve over time. They are created and sustained by those who are in power, generally the dominant group within the organization. Leaders are often the curators of the culture. Founders of organizations define the expectations for the organization and these values and edicts continue on as individuals of like mind are recruited and promoted into leadership. Hence, I often hear leadership teams debating on whether or not someone fits within the organizational culture when they are contemplating bringing in new talent.

Organizations' leaders generally adopt one of three approaches either to maintain the status quo within the culture or to enable it to be enriched by difference. The philosophy and approaches used are typically either assimilation, pluralism, or multiculturalism.[2]

Assimilation demands the most conformity and requires that individuals take on the characteristics of and adapt to the norms of the dominant group. This may result in certain individuals foregoing expression of their own cultural upbringing. Assimilation into the organizational culture is generally facilitated through orientation, onboarding, values, and culture training, and the key messages that are embedded in these forums. One might also be assigned a mentor or buddy who can help a newbie by providing feedback and enabling them to course-correct if they notice them demonstrating countercultural behaviors. Assimilation is also reinforced in the performance management, rewards, promotion, and progressive disciplinary systems.

Pluralism is another mindset and approach that is taken by organizations. Pluralism recognizes and values the unique cultural identities within various groups and strives to put into place policies, practices, and structures that enable smaller groups to maintain and express these identities. In a pluralist culture, groups not only coexist side by side but also consider qualities of other groups as traits worth having in the dominant culture. Pluralistic organizations place strong expectations of integration on members, rather than expectations of assimilation. An example in the workplace would be the establishment and sponsorship of Employee Resource Groups, the acknowledgment and celebration of histories and accomplishments of several groups, and forums for facilitating cross-generational, cross-functional, and cross-demographic collaborations.

Multiculturalism lacks the requirement of a dominant culture. Cultural pluralism is distinct from multiculturalism. If the dominant culture of a society or organization is weak, smaller groups can contribute relatively equally to the prevailing culture. While many organizations indicate this is a desired state, this is actually very challenging to facilitate.

Pressures to Conform

I remember having a conversation with a colleague when I was aspiring to advance. I was looking for his insights and feedback. What he said took me aback. He said, "Well Tyronne you don't really fit in with the image of an executive." I was thinking, "What do you mean I don't fit?" A shoe that's too large doesn't fit. A tight sweater doesn't fit. He said, "Well you don't dress like an executive; and you don't really look like the typical executive. For example, you have facial hair"

At that point, I could feel the hairs on the back of my neck standing at attention!

I was proud of my mustache. It took me decades to get it to the point it was at at that time. Heck, I received compliments all the time on my mustache. And *this* was a barrier to me advancing? What did my mustache have to do with my competency level, my performance, or the outcomes I was achieving within the organization. In my opinion, my record spoke for itself.

So, I began to do some exploring on my own. I looked at all the newscasters, primarily Black male newscasters, and noticed they didn't have any mustaches or beards. I looked at former and current politicians, including President Obama, and noticed he didn't have a beard. I looked at my mentor, John Rogers, and noticed he didn't have any facial hair. Maybe there's something to this. I must have missed the memo along my career that made this explicit. So, I decided to assimilate. I shaved my mustache. I started wearing khakis, white shirts, and blue blazers. And if you know me at all, you know that is not my go-to style.

I have shared that story in meetings and presentations and have found that others have felt the same pressure to conform. Women who had worn their natural hairstyles and braids went back to straightening their hair. Men shaved their mustaches and beards and came out of their budget for a new wardrobe. In some companies where leadership becomes aware of this, I have noticed that they take steps to challenge the culture. For example, leaders have initiated and/or condoned grassroots efforts like a "beard challenge" where the men in the company grow back their beards to visibly advocate for a change in cultural norms. This is a wonderful example of how Ah Ha moments and leadership intervention can change aspects of the culture allowing people to bring their authentic selves into the workplace.

Often when individuals are looking for work, they are also looking for an organization whose values, assumptions, and beliefs align with their own. What happens when there is a mismatch between the culture and the individual?

Assimilation vs. Acculturation

Acculturation is the process whereby an individual from one cultural group learns and adopts elements of another cultural group, integrating them into their original culture. Although it can refer to any process of cultural integration, it is typically used to describe the ways in which an immigrant or marginalized group adopts cultural elements from the mainstream culture.

Assimilation is one outcome of acculturation. It involves the complete adoption of the behaviors, values, norms, and beliefs of the dominant cultural group, resulting in the assimilated group losing nearly all of its original or native culture. Organizations often sanction assimilation but use acculturation as a more sanitized term for it. Individuals in underrepresented groups will consent to assimilation by minimizing their authentic identities. This includes a range of actions including changing one's name, appearance, communication style, and behaviors.

For example, research has shown that resumes on which foreign or more ethnic-sounding names appear are less likely to be included in the next hurdle of the selection process. Consequently, you will find individuals who are migrating from other countries or U.S. citizens who happen to have more ethnic-sounding names like Lashawn, Javier, or Tyronne often representing themselves with shorter nicknames like Sean, Jack, or Ty. This is a strategy of trying to "fit in" to "get in."

Emphasis on everyone being the same puts pressure on employees to make sure that important differences and different perspectives do not count. Disagreements are seen as violating the code of assimilation. Conflict is suppressed and people feel alienated. This suboptimizes individual performance and an organization's capacity to learn about and improve its practices.

Biculturalism and Code-Switching

Biculturalism occurs when an individual acquires and displays the identity and behaviors of both their own culture and the mainstream culture. They are generally capable of effective interactions in both settings. This is often achieved through code-switching.

We behave differently at work, with friends, and with our family members. This code-switching involves adapting our behavior (either consciously or unconsciously) to match that of the dominant group. The term code-switching was originally documented by sociologist John J. Gumperz and it was used to describe a linguistic phenomenon in which a person alternates between two or more languages or dialects within a single conversation.[3] Today it has been discussed as a survival strategy for marginalized groups and manifests in dressing the part, trying to look the part, talking like "them," and engaging in hobbies like "them."

Now granted, part of this may just be adopting a more professional demeanor when we are in the workplace. We will adapt to different behaviors depending on the context or situation. If we are on the phone trying to make a sale to a potential customer, we may use our professional phone voice. If we're on the phone with our BFF, we will most likely be more colloquial and relaxed. It is human nature to want to be viewed as fitting in. The danger occurs when our contextual identities are out of step with our authentic identities. This is when we are not necessarily choosing to adapt because of the situation but feel compelled to suppress aspects of ourselves.

This shift might manifest as an employee from, let's say, Birmingham, who is proud of his southern roots and dialect, moving to Boston and noticing some of the odd stares he receives during his presentations. He often gets comments like "What did you say? Could you repeat that? I can't quite understand you." He also notices that he has been left off of emails where informal get-togethers have been planned during business trips and conferences. He begins to question his credibility as he feels he is always being scrutinized and judged. He works diligently on suppressing his dialect to sound more like an easterner and takes up golf, which he actually deplores, in order to connect with individuals considered part of the inner circle.

Sometimes we are switching and not even understanding the reasons why we're doing so. I'm reminded of this video clip I saw where a man was getting ready to get on an elevator. The elevator door opens and there are four men standing in the elevator with coats and hats on facing him. The man has a coat and hat on as well. When the elevator gets to its designated floor the door opens again and we notice that the original group of four men who were on the elevator have turned to face the back of the elevator and have taken their hats off. The man who entered last has also done the same.

Now this may sound like an exaggerated example, but it shows the power of the dominant group in driving behavior change. We will often try to match the norms of the environment that we're in even when we don't understand them. With code-switching we have learned to do so with such fluidity that we may not even recognize that we're doing it.

Active Resistance

Someone who feels that their authentic identity is being compromised at work may choose to actively resist. They may call folks on the carpet every opportunity they get. They may choose to ignore norms around the hierarchy, communication, and anything that might suggest how they should look or dress. Many of these behaviors might be viewed as innocuous to their performance or to the company's performance. However, decisions made about this individual may impact them adversely. Because they are viewed as rocking the boat, not a team player, and not trying to demonstrate the company's values, this may result in them being passed over for projects or promotions.

Active resistance does not have to be aggressive. For example, I do not drink alcohol, nor do I smoke. Often, though, I am in the company of individuals who suggest getting together after business hours to go to a cigar bar or unwind over drinks. I let them know right away that I don't mind coming with you, but I don't drink or smoke.

Some people are offended by this. I get bewildered stares. But that does not change my behavior. I grew up with a family member who was an alcoholic and I have intentionally chosen not to drink. Additionally, I don't feel the need to drink to feel more comfortable within a group setting. I have no qualms against others who do so. But I feel no pressure at all to compromise my position or my health by trying to "fit in" in this particular situation.

Is there a consequence to this? There might be. A lot of important business decisions are discussed in bars over drinks. A lot of promotion opportunities are presented on golf courses. I may be excluded from certain communications or external activities. There often is a price to pay for choosing to stand by your principles and honoring your authentic self. But you'll probably be able to sleep better at night knowing that you did so.

Passive Resistance and Quiet Quitting

An individual also may challenge the culture in more passive ways that are not that detectable to those who are keepers of the culture. They may withhold information they know that others need because they don't agree with how projects have been assigned. They may spread gossip that speaks disparagingly of leadership or others who they feel are blocking their careers. They might call in sick on a holiday that is not celebrated by the organization. They may use sarcasm or humor in meetings to challenge a point with which they don't agree. Passive resistance often aligns with quiet quitting.

Quiet quitting occurs when employees put in the minimal effort needed to hold on to their jobs. They are not engaged. They are not willing to do anything extra; they certainly aren't ambassadors for their employers. This terminology became popular during the COVID-19 pandemic as employees began to reassess their jobs and their value. Feeling that you do not fit in with the culture, that you don't belong, can lead to turning things down a notch.

Separation

There's always the probability that individuals who do not feel they fit in respond by leaving the organization. This could be either a win-win or a win-lose. If the individual's authentic style and values truly clash with the values of the organization, then it might be good for both parties to separate. This would be beneficial for the employees leaving as they would not have to experience the cognitive dissonance of trying to present themselves in a way that does not align with their authenticity. It would be a win-lose if this separation damaged the reputation of the individual or the organization. It would also be a loss for the organization if there were adaptations that could have been made to retain a key performer.

Minimization: Going Along to Get Along

I leverage the Intercultural Development Inventory (IDI) quite a bit in the work I do to assess the level of cross-cultural competency on leadership teams. Within organizations, the majority of individuals and teams that take this assessment fall within the minimization orientation (close to 70% across industries). Minimization is *"An orientation that highlights cultural commonality and universal values and principles that may also mask deeper recognition and appreciation of cultural differences."*[4]

The literature supporting the IDI tells us that organizations whose leadership teams are in minimization will tend to implement one-size-fits-all practices and policies, focusing on what employees have in common. This is done with the intent of being fair and consistent. They may have a false sense of implementing practices that they feel support equality, when they should be focusing on understanding the nuanced needs of different groups in order to promote equity. One-sized solutions do not promote equity.

Those in minimization are described as "bridge builders." That is, they facilitate employee connections and highlight commonalities on their teams. This is beneficial when you are bringing polarized groups together. However, if members of each polarized group still harbor biases or stereotypes, focus solely on commonality, and don't learn to value the power of differences, then the work of unifying teams is only partially done. This feeling of unity most likely will not translate into other situations.

When I am debriefing and coaching individuals who are in minimization that happen to be part of a marginalized group, a main motivator for them doing so is that they don't want to stand out, they go along to get along. They are not trying to draw attention to their difference, and so in turn, they assimilate into the dominant culture often minimizing authentic aspects of their personalities or experience.

Authenticity: A Game of Bait and Switch

Organizations bring in leaders for their skill and experience and add that "we want you to bring your full, authentic self! We are looking for diverse perspectives." Flash back to the earlier scenario involving Alejandro. But if you come in with an idea that is too novel or your approach does not align, you're told that "this is not the XYZ Company way."

We end up hanging our unique strengths and capabilities on the coat rack at the office door and operating with a fixed mindset. This downplaying of our capabilities fuels the mindset that we were "just affirmative action hires anyway" and contributes to the self-fulfilling prophecy that we aren't as qualified or skilled. Suppressing our personal identities limits the level of trust we can build in our relationships. Individuals will tend to speculate about what we are holding back.

In a study conducted by Job Sage, results showed that:

- More than three in five respondents admitted to hiding something from their current employer. Most often, they hide political views (37%) and information about their family (36%). They do so to avoid making people uncomfortable (49%), avoid stereotyping (43%), and out of fear that it might impact their career advancement (41%). Fifty-five percent reported that this effort has an adverse effect on mental health.
- Even though respondents value being authentic, most said they still hide or alter some aspect of their lives, with seven in 10 reporting that they adopt a different personality at work than they do at home. Even those who weren't hiding or altering some aspect of their identity still needed a while to be themselves, with one in five saying they needed at least six months to feel comfortable being authentic.[5]

Sustaining this suppressing behavior can be an emotional toll for employees. Additionally, coworkers and managers do not really get to know or benefit from the real you. You can't wait till 5:30 p.m. or the weekend so you can take off your cloak. You dread Monday morning, because you have to put it on again. You are always on stage yet the real you is invisible!

As an example, I have observed that my White colleagues have questioned things that are a normal part of my life outside of work. For example, I attend and am a Deacon at a large Black church, located in

Chicago. And as part of that, the congregation is pretty much like my family. So, when a prominent member of the church passes away, I go to the funeral. And because the church is so large, I am often attending funeral services more than once a month. When I share this with my White colleagues, their reaction is "Wow, Tyronne you go to a lot of funerals! What is wrong? Why is everybody around you dying?"

They view what is happening in my world as being some sort of deficit or abnormality. But I was raised to have a close relationship with my congregation, that you participate and visibly support them as they are going through challenges or other milestones within their lives. I stopped sharing these parts of my personal life with my colleagues and felt I needed to shrink myself or minimize my experience in order to fit in. I still do not share as much today, as I know this leads to others judging me on things they can't relate to because it is not a part of their experience.

According to a 2022 *Forbes* article, this inauthentic expression is an issue for leaders. But leaders can role model authenticity by making genuine connections with their employees. One manager offered:

> I don't pretend to check my "real life" at the door just because I am the boss and, in doing so, I make it clear to my employees that I don't expect them to either. Authenticity is a two-way street; by allowing both sides of the employer-employee relationship to bring their whole self to work, we create space for all parties to thrive.
>
> . . . [E]mployees are more likely to share their honest thoughts and feedback with leaders when they have formed a genuine connection with them and trust their thoughts will be heard with an open mind.[6]

While individuals will want to bring their authentic selves to work, it needs to be done within the scope of the professional business culture. And I believe it does not require one to be disingenuous to do so.

It may require emotional intelligence, specifically, self-awareness and self-management. Some might argue that there is a thin line between authentic behavior and unprofessional behavior. Leadership can help redefine that boundary.

Leadership and Culture Change

Speaking of leadership, think about a time when you experienced or observed inclusive leadership. What was it about the experience that you most noted or admired? Did you observe the leader making an effort to make sure everyone was heard? Did you see them encouraging their team to be innovative and take calculated risks? Did you notice that they admitted that there was something they just didn't know and were open to other perspectives? How did they hold others accountable for supporting an inclusive environment?

Organizational culture is inseparable from its leadership. They have a primary role in creating, sustaining, and rebuilding culture. This is done through the leader's ongoing communications, advocacy, sponsorship, and through their personal interactions with others. It becomes institutionalized through the strategies, systems, policies, and practices they endorse. Culture is perpetuated through what leaders hold their direct reports accountable for and through which behaviors are rewarded.

Because of their powerful influence on how culture manifests, it is critical that leaders possess awareness of their own assumptions, beliefs, and values.

An Ah Ha Moment!

I have had conversations with several CEOs and executives where I observed Ah Ha moments once they became aware of their value system and how it was or was not demonstrated in the work they were responsible for. I recall one conversation with an executive of a large financial institution. I really liked his personality. He was approachable, had a big-picture vision, and supported the DEI efforts within his organization, at least on the surface. I was there to debrief him on his IDI results. His score was in an IDI orientation stage, labeled "polarization," that he did not like, and he said to me, "So, you're here to tell me that I'm a racist. I don't believe that. That's not what I stand for." I said, "Your results do not imply that you are a racist but that you take an evaluative approach when you look at people from different cultural backgrounds and assume that your life experience and values are better than theirs. But before we go down this path any further, look at those two young ladies in the portrait on your credenza. I'm assuming they are your daughters." He acknowledged that they were. I asked how and what they were doing, and he let me know that they were in business school.

I then said, "So what are you going to say to them when they graduate from business school and come into the workplace? What are you going to tell them about how they will be treated, that women typically face a glass ceiling when they try to advance into leadership. But more importantly, how are you going to explain to them that you had a chance to close that gap for women in your organization, but you hesitated?"

Ah Ha! That resonated! It enabled him to think about his role differently. He was so inspired by this conversation that he became very actively involved. This resulted in one of his mentees of color being promoted to a top executive position within the institution.

When we look at how leaders can create a culture, it helps when they can personalize it. They will continue to think of people as "others" if they do not look like them or don't enter the organization through the same channels. Leaders begin to look at things differently when the impacts of a discriminating or toxic work culture affect someone close to them. It helps them to understand their biases, their resistance, and build empathy, but it also shows them where there are opportunities and the role that they can play in initiating change.

Change can start with one conversation!

Creating or rebuilding an inclusive culture is no small undertaking. There are several considerations and approaches that have been associated with successfully transforming culture. In my work as a DEI practitioner, I have found that organizations that are progressively working to build and sustain inclusive cultures do so based on certain foundational principles and behaviors. These include leadership visibility, holistic strategies, transparent communication, stakeholder engagement, accountability systems, commitment, and the ability to press on or pivot when needed. My "Call to Action" for leaders follows.

Think Holistically and Systemically

Culture is embedded in people, policies, practices, and processes. Attempts to change the culture need to address all of these components. Culture change involves many conversations with many individuals. It should reflect an understanding of how the culture is viewed and experienced by different stakeholder groups. This can facilitate the creation of a shared vision that aligns with the business mission. Culture change imperatives should be outlined in a strategy document that is detailed, yet dynamic to account for greater changes in the business environment.

Get Out of the Tower!

Executives are often insulated from the day-to-day culture. Their view of the impacts of culture, policies, and practices is often nearsighted. This narrow view limits the extent to which relevant and supportive systems can be developed.

I am a strong proponent of "managing by walking around" as well as scheduling informal fireside chats. It benefits me by providing me with a more complete picture of the organization, and also sends a message to others that I am accessible. In my current role, I could not be effective unless I was aware of the challenges and opportunities of our employees, customers, and communities in our different regions. So, you will find me on a flight to Hong Kong, Sweden, Dubai, D.C., or the Bahamas within the span of a month. I benefit by seeing things first-hand. This role modeling of behavior helps to build trust and is often mimicked by other leaders and managers who observe it.

Get into the Weeds to Acknowledge What Is Flourishing

What beliefs, behaviors, and practices need to be uprooted; what new seeds need to be planted, and what plants are already flourishing and need to be maintained? That is the question! Changing the culture does not always require a complete overhaul nor does it require boiling the ocean and trying to do everything at once. Organizations should be reminded to build on their current strengths. Specific departments or teams may be more proactive than others in creating cultures that are inclusive. Leaders can use appreciative inquiry by looking at segments of the organization that are doing well, where inclusion and equity are evident, where employees from diverse backgrounds are engaged, retained, and advancing. What is unique about these business units and how can the rest of the organization learn from them?

Engage All Levels

A critical part of a senior executive's success in transforming culture hinges on their ability to engage other leaders in the change process. This can be done by including them in planning conversations, creating developmental assignments like ERG sponsorship, DEI Council participation, and mentorship. Each leader has an opportunity, and I would argue, accountability, to present themselves as a champion for change and advocate for DEI. They can solicit multiple insights and share how their specific business units and teams experience the culture, provide suggestions for improvement, and help shape a vision for moving forward. Managers and supervisors can encourage authentic expression by modeling it. This will contribute exponentially to creating a culture of transparency and trust.

The dysfunction on diverse teams can be mitigated by effective management practices and collective commitment from team members. Additionally, self-awareness tools that help team members learn about their own and others' work and communication styles can be administered. Managers can remind their teams that a learning mindset, risk tolerance, open-mindedness, and a willingness to address conflict within safe spaces are all relevant to creating an optimal team culture for inclusion and equity.

In tandem, leaders can leverage surveys and focus groups to ensure that the voice of the employee, customer, and community are heard and embedded into the vision for change. Soliciting and leveraging multiple perspectives will help leaders gain insights, experience Ah Ha moments, and build empathy.

Create a Culture of Mentoring and Sponsorship

Sponsors and mentors can have a significant impact on individuals who feel disconnected from the culture. Mentors can provide insight into the spoken and unspoken rules of the culture and can help employees expand their networks. Providing this support, particularly to new hires who are challenged with navigating the culture, can minimize the revolving door syndrome. I must admit that many of my mentors came from outside of my organizations. Yet I gained invaluable insights from them that helped me in the workplace as well as in the community. I also believe that leaders should actively discuss sponsorship, identify areas or groups for which there is a gap, and take action to reconcile this. My story about the executive who had an Ah Ha moment during his IDI debrief shows how quickly one can transition from being just a mentor to being a sponsor.

Distribute Accountability

To make and sustain progress on culture change, all levels of management and all employees must feel a sense of ownership. Culture change cannot be abdicated to one functional area or one level. Granted, all employees need to understand what is expected of them and how this relates to their role. Leaders must be willing to establish metrics, performance goals, bonus contingencies, and ask tough questions to ensure that their teams are on track. Reinforcement and recognition can be utilized for those who are resisting as well as for those who are changing the game.

Adopt a Long-Term View

Organizational culture is generally strongly rooted and difficult to change. The path to change will not always be linear. It may look more like a roller coaster ride. Behaviors and practices that are steeped in culture often occur on autopilot. It may take a few seasons for change to sink in, but ongoing persistence and an infrastructure that supports DEI will help organizations turn the tide. Leaders must be committed to the long term and find ways to celebrate incremental progress. These little wins can inspire and lead to transformational change!

Tactical Tools/Considerations

In the sections in this chapter, I have suggested ways that leaders can lead culture change within their organizations. I outline the points made earlier here as well as add suggestions for individual contributors.

Individuals can:

- Build social networks both within and outside of the organization where you can express your authentic identities.

- Seek insight from individuals from different backgrounds to gain insight on authentic ways to navigate the organizational culture.
- Share your concerns and or experiences with individuals you trust.
- Pose questions about the organizational culture to those who are currently employed as well as to former employees to determine if the espoused values match behaviors and practices.
- Take ownership for your professional growth and pursue activities, or educational experiences that will empower you and keep you marketable.
- While it takes courage and there is some risk, challenge practices in a respectful way when you feel they compromise your work experience.

Organizational leaders and practitioners can:

- Think holistically and systemically.
- Get out of the tower!
- Get into the weeds to acknowledge what is flourishing.
- Engage all levels.
- Create a culture of mentoring and sponsorship.
- Distribute accountability.
- Adopt a long-term view.

8

Change Starts With You!

"These Are a Few of My Favorite Things . . ."

I want to share with you some of my favorite frameworks and activities. Frameworks provide us with a common language to understand our behaviors and actions and to gauge where we are making progress and where further improvements are needed. These frameworks have been invaluable in the conversations I have held with other leaders, when I am keynoting within a conference room of 1,000 people, and in my personal interactions outside of work. I have discussed some of these frameworks and tools throughout the book, while others will appear here for the first time. But I am presenting all of them here as a unified collection for your easy reference.

The Power of Ah Ha Moments

I like to use this framework to emphasize that Leadership can have a significant impact on institutionalized practices that are inequitable. They are a driving force in changing culture and systems. It often starts with Ah Ha or light bulb moments. When leaders receive specific feedback that does not mesh with their assumptions, it provides an opportunity for them to self-correct. This feedback might come through a survey or from an Employee Resource Group that speaks to how an organizational practice has disparate impacts for specific groups. When these conditions are present a leader can then use their position and power to advocate for and influence change within others and within various organizational systems (see Figure 8.1).

Johari's Window (Joseph Luft & Harry Ingham)[1]

In my presentations and coaching discussions with leaders, I often talk about blind spots. When we offend someone or perhaps overlook the

189

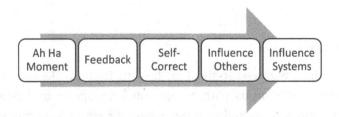

FIGURE 8.1 "Ah Ha" moments framework.

needs or issues of those around us, it may be because we don't know what we don't know. This is a blind spot. Johari's window has been used extensively in organizational development and training to provide common language for this. As depicted in Figure 8.2, there are some things that both we and others know about us. It might be a demonstrated strength—that we are a great communicator. There are things that we know about ourselves that others don't. This might be some latent talent or aspirational goal that we have that we have not shared. There are also things that others know about us, but we don't seem to get. These are our blind spots. I find that a good way to keep a pulse on these blind spots is to seek feedback from others, or to participate in assessments like the IDI. Finally, there are things that neither we nor others know

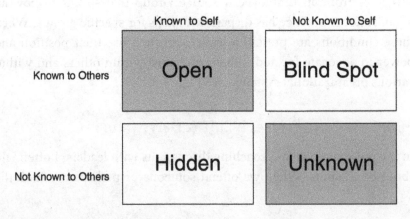

FIGURE 8.2 Johari's Window.

about us until a situation calls for it. It could manifest as a coworker remaining calm and guiding everyone out of the building during a threatening situation.

Ladder of Inference (Chris Argyris, Peter Senge)[2,3]

This model (see Figure 8.3) provides a mental tool for helping us to avoid assumptions and stereotypes. This is especially relevant when we are in a new or uncomfortable situation or engaging with someone we don't know well. It provides a process for us to follow if we tend to make a decision based on limited data. The goal is to reflect on what we are observing in a situation and what assumptions we are drawing from it. Assumptions are often based on the implicit biases we hold. Instead of immediately taking action, we need to challenge ourselves to be more curious and seek more data before arriving at conclusions and making a decision. For example, we may jump to the top rung of the ladder in an interview with someone who has come to the organization through a nontraditional recruitment source (let's say an HBCU). Our bias might lead us to draw conclusions that they aren't as qualified or well-networked as the Ivy League candidates, and so we don't take the time to gather sufficient data before making a decision not to hire.

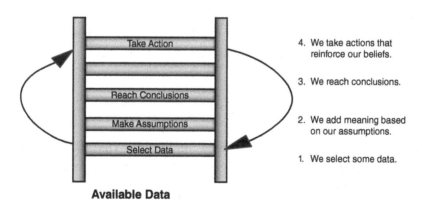

FIGURE 8.3 Ladder of inference.

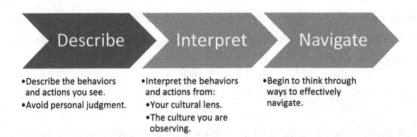

FIGURE 8.4 Describe, interpret, navigate (D.I.N.) model.

D.I.N. Model

This framework (see Figure 8.4) is widely used by practitioners (Describe, Interpret, Navigate) to provide a process for thinking through our assumptions before we take action. I described it in Chapter 6, Stereotypes.

The trainer provides a scenario or skit in which a complex cultural situation is played out. It might include two participants acting out an argument. I've also seen a skit that showed a woman walking behind a man into the room, kneeling down at his feet while he ate from a bowl, and then share it with her. Participants will often skip the Describe step and jump to Interpretation saying things like, "The man feels he is superior to the woman. He is making her sit on the ground and eat leftovers." Depending on one's culture, the scenario might actually reflect a man coming into the room to make sure there is no danger, enabling the woman to sit on the ground because it is more sacred to be closer to the earth, and testing the food before he gives it to her to make sure it is safe to eat!

The Developmental Model of Intercultural Sensitivity (Milton Bennett, Mitchell Hammer)[5,6]

The Developmental Model of Intercultural Sensitivity (DMIS) represents various orientations that reflect how we respond to cultural differences (see Figure 8.5).

The Intercultural Development Inventory (IDI) was developed to measure where a person falls on the DMIS continuum. It is a very effective

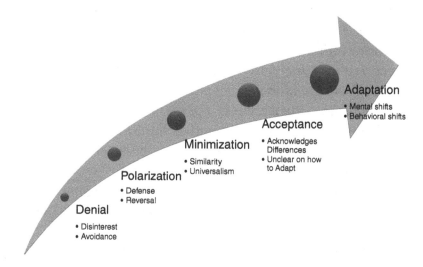

FIGURE 8.5 The developmental model of intercultural sensitivity.

tool for creating common language within an organization and coaching leaders and employees. I use this extensively in my work with leadership teams. The IDI is a premier cross-cultural assessment. It has been demonstrated, through research, to have high predictive validity to both bottom-line cross-cultural outcomes in organizations and intercultural goal accomplishments in education. A brief description of each orientation on the continuum is provided in the Intercultural Development Inventory sidebar.

The Intercultural Development Inventory

- **Denial:** *An orientation that recognizes more observable cultural differences (e.g., food), but may not notice deeper cultural difference (e.g., conflict resolution styles) and may avoid or withdraw from such differences*
- **Polarization:** *A judgmental orientation that views cultural difference in terms of "us" and "them" This ranges from (1) a more*

> uncritical view toward one's own cultural values and practices coupled with an overly critical view toward other cultural values and practices (<u>Defense</u>) to (2) an overly critical orientation toward one's own cultural values and practices and an uncritical view toward other cultural values and practices (<u>Reversal</u>).
>
> - **Minimization:** An orientation that highlights cultural commonality and universal values and principles that may also mask deeper recognition and appreciation of cultural differences.
> - **Acceptance:** An orientation that recognizes and appreciates patterns of cultural difference and commonality in one's own and other cultures.
> - **Adaptation:** An orientation that can shift cultural perspective and change behavior in culturally appropriate and authentic ways.

The Seven Dimensions of Culture (Trompenaars and Hampden-Turner)[7]

Trompenaars and Hampden-Turner's framework provides seven dimensions that can be used to help understand cultural differences across businesses, industries, and nations.

The Seven Dimensions of Culture

- **Relationships and Rules (Universal versus the Particular)** – Universalism basically asserts that what is good and right always applies, while particularism puts more weight on the unique situation and obligation to relationships.
- **The Group and the Individual (Individualism vs. Communitarianism)** – The contrast between these two

dimensions is anchored in whether we put ourselves as a person first in a group, or whether we put the importance of the group first.

- **Feelings and Relationships (Affective vs. Neutral)** – This juxtaposition looks at the extent to which we feel expressing emotions is acceptable or whether our interactions should be objective and detached.
- **How Far We Get Involved (Specific vs. Diffuse)** – The Specific orientation suggests that you limit your interactions with others to particular contexts (e.g., at work only). The Diffuse cultural orientation would be one in which you feel it is preferable to engage with individuals in many aspects of your life, both professional and personal.
- **How We Accord Status (Achievement vs. Ascription)** – We judge individuals on their record of accomplishments in Achievement and on things that are attributable to aspects like birth, kinship and other relationships, gender, age, and credentials.
- **How We Manage Time (Sequential vs. Synchronic)** – In Sequential cultures, the emphasis is on completing tasks in discrete elements, one by one, with a clear start and finish. In Synchronic cultures, past and present are fused together and there is more tolerance to interruptions of the sequence. For example, someone with a synchronic orientation might feel very comfortable interrupting a business meeting to take a call from a relative who had just arrived in town.
- **How We Relate to Nature (Internal vs. External Control)** – Specific cultures view the major impacts on their life as being within their internal control while other cultures view nature or external events in the world as being more powerful and something to be revered or feared.

Six Dimensions of Culture (Geert Hofstede)[8]

Geert Hofstede developed a similar model for describing cultural differences within and across societies and organizations. This is widely used in industry and academia and is based on substantive research. His six dimensions of culture are described in the Six Dimensions of Culture sidebar.

The Six Dimensions of Culture

- **Power Distance Index (PDI)** is the extent to which the less powerful members of organizations and institutions accept and expect that power is distributed unequally.
- **Individualism (IDV)** versus collectivism is the degree to which individuals are integrated into groups. Those from collectivist cultures tend to emphasize relationships and loyalty more than those from individualistic cultures.
- **Masculinity (MAS)** versus femininity refers to the distribution of roles between the genders. A masculine society values assertiveness, courage, strength, and competition. A feminine society values cooperation, nurturing, and quality of life.
- A high **Uncertainty Avoidance Index (UAI)** indicates a low tolerance for uncertainty, ambiguity, and risk-taking. In contrast, those in low uncertainty avoidance cultures accept and feel comfortable in unstructured situations or changeable environments and try to have as few rules as possible.
- **Long-Term Orientation (LTO)** societies tend to focus on the future in a way that delays short-term success in favor of success in the long term. Short-term orientation indicates a focus on the near future and involves delivering short-term success or gratification.
- **Restraint vs. Indulgence** looks at the extent and tendency of a society to fulfill its desires. In a highly indulgent

---

society, people tend to spend more money on luxuries and enjoy more freedom when it comes to leisure time activities. In a restrained society, people are more likely to save money and focus on practical needs.

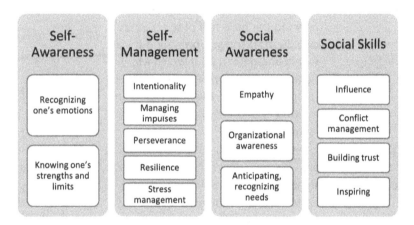

FIGURE 8.6 Emotional intelligence framework.

Emotional Intelligence (Mayer & Salovey, Goleman)[9,10]

There is significant alignment between EQ frameworks and cross-cultural competency. As Figure 8.6 depicts, there are several components to EQ. What I especially like about this framework is the focus on both awareness and skill.

Check Your Language

We often don't know what we don't know. One example is the use of language and colloquial phrases used regularly in our conversations. The list in the following table is just a sample of some of the common terms that have racist or sexist origins or associations. Facilitators can incorporate this into discussions on culture or bias. The objective is to

raise awareness, not to point fingers, as many of us use these phrases
without any intent to harm.

Common Phrase	Origin or Association	Alternative Option
As pleased as Punch!	Based on Punch and Judy Puppet Shows from sixteenth-century Italy. Punch refers to the male half of the puppet duo. In most shows, something trivial would enrage him after which Mr. Punch would go on a murderous rampage, kill Judy, their baby, and any interfering authority figure and then laugh about it.	Very pleased
Blackball; Black mark	The use of "black" to describe things that are wrong is subconsciously racialized.	Shut out; Issue of concern
Cakewalk	Originated as a dance performed by enslaved Black people on plantations before the Civil War.	Easy victory/ win
Dreadlocks; Dreads	There are potential negative connotations to fear or dread when using this termi-nology for the hairstyle.	Locs
Gypped	Comes from the word "Gypsy," which is a derogatory name for the Romani people.	Cheated; Ripped off
Hip Hip Hooray!	Thought to have come from the anti-Semitic chant "Hep hep!" which was a rallying cry to attack Jewish people during the German Confederacy. At some point, "hep hep" became "hip hip," and "hooray" was added to the end.	Just use Hooray or Yay
Low-hanging fruit	Referenced in song lyrics (Billie Holiday's "Strange Fruit") to Black men and women who were lynched and hanging low from tree branches.	Easy win or quick hit
Master bedroom	It suggests references to slavery on plantations.	Primary

Common Phrase	Origin or Association	Alternative Option
Master/slave	Used to describe components of software and hardware in which one process or device controls another.	Parent/child or primary/ secondary
Paddy wagon	This nineteenth-century slang referenced Irish immigrants who upon being arrested were put in a police van, called a paddy wagon. Reinforces drunken or unruly stereotypes.	Police van
Peanut gallery	The peanut gallery was the cheapest section of seats (hence classist or racist). Peanuts were sold at these shows, which would sometimes be thrown at unpopular performers.	Critics or hecklers
Rule of thumb	Surfaced in the 1700s, during which time British common law permitted a man to beat his wife as long as the rod used was no thicker than his thumb.	Guiding principle

Activities and Demonstrations

A picture is worth 1,000 words. An experience is worth a million. I have used immersion activities and demonstrations to help drive home a point for the many clients and audiences with whom I engage. A couple of exercises that I have found to be invaluable to build Ah Ha moments and empathy are described next.

Dining in the Dark: Building Empathy Through Blindfolds[11]

In this activity a group of individuals is taken to a restaurant. Prior to them entering and being seated, they will be asked to put on blindfolds.

They are then expected to make it to their seats and tables with a little bit of help so that they don't knock anything over or harm themselves. Then they are tasked with ordering a meal and eating it. As you might imagine, this is very difficult for someone who is sighted and used to seeing what they are doing. Glasses fall; food goes places other than intended. Those participating often become very frustrated. After the meal is over and they are able to take off their blindfolds, they now learn that the waitstaff who were serving them consisted of individuals who were vision-impaired. In this exercise, participants realize how much is required for someone who is not able to see. This Ah Ha moment brings appreciation for the privileges we take for granted and builds empathy for others.

The Walk of Privilege[12]

This is another activity I like to facilitate to start a discussion on group inequities. I will ask individuals to stand in a line. I will then give basic instructions. For each one for which an individual can respond affirmatively, they can take a step forward. If their answer is "no" they have to take a step backward. The instructions are things like:

- If you are right-handed, take a step forward.
- If you can trace your ancestral roots back to a specific country, take a step forward.
- If your parents and grandparents went to college take a step forward.
- If you rely on public transportation, take a step back.
- If you grew up in a single-parent household, take a step back.
- If you have ever faced sexual harassment at the workplace, take a step back.

By the end of this exercise, participants can look around the room and note who is ahead and who is behind. If it is a diverse group, you will typically see White males at the front of the line with White women following and participants of color closer to the back. I have found this to be a very effective and visible way to begin the discussion on privilege.

Continuing Your Journey

There are numerous frameworks and activities that are relevant to DEI and creating culture change. I invite you to find at least two or three ways in which you can leverage from those presented in this chapter and apply them to your professional and personal lives.

I find that the more we engage in our learning the more new concepts will take hold and be internalized. Being a collaborator in our development versus simply listening to others is empowering. It helps us identify our strengths. It creates Ah Ha moments that challenge our assumptions. This can help minimize our resistance to change. And if I haven't said it enough, this book is all about change. It starts with me. It starts with you. It starts right now!

Call to Action

So, this is the final chapter, but it is not the end. In each of the preceding chapters I have provided information, insights, and my personal experiences on a number of topics that relate to diverse, equitable, and inclusive workplaces. I also shared some of the broader societal and historical factors that have implications for how groups engage within the workplace. In this chapter, I shared and reintroduced some of my favorite frameworks and activities.

I wrestled with the title for this book. I wanted it to reflect the outlandish incidents that I have witnessed and been subjected to in my life and how this relates to the work that I am very passionate about now. As I thought about these incidents, what came to mind were several four-letter words. My publisher gently guided me out of that space. But I also thought of how I have experienced, observed, and modeled other four-letter words like "care" and "ally," along with "empathy," "compassion," and "action." I chose not to have this book be all about rage and insidious acts but to highlight these examples so that I could transition the discussion to one of more hope and action. I trust that this book has shown that balance.

As you were reading, I would anticipate that you had some Ah Ha moments or were reminded of principles you may not have thought about in a while. I imagine that practitioners reading this will find many areas that resonate with the work that they are doing. My hope is that you will go back to chapters that resonate, share with your teams, and, more importantly, decide how you can make a difference in your day to day. Knowledge without action has no life. If it only has residence inside of your head, it cannot make a difference.

So, let's make a pact and breathe life into this book. Let's take the words beyond the pages and into the workplace. Each of us can impact change. We can truly be the change we want to see in the world. Change Starts With You!

I wish all of you the best on your personal and professional journeys. Until we meet again.

Inclusively yours,

Tyronne

Notes

Chapter 1

1. Winters, M.-F. (2002). *Only Wet Babies Like Change: Workplace Wisdom for Baby Boomers.* Charlotte, NC: Winters Group, Inc.
2. Trompenaars, F. and Hampden-Turner, C. (1998). *Riding the Waves of Culture.* New York: McGraw-Hill.
3. Hofstede, G. (n.d.). The 6-D Model of National Culture. https://geerthofstede.com/culture-geert-hofstede-gert-jan-hofstede/6d-model-of-national-culture/.
4. Hammer, M.R., Bennett, M.J., and Wiseman, R. (2003). Measuring intercultural sensitivity: The Intercultural Development Inventory. *International Journal of Intercultural Relations* 27 (4): 421–443. https://doi.org/10.1016/S0147-1767(03)00032-4.
5. Hammer, M.R. (n.d.). Intercultural Development Inventory. https://www.idiinventory.com/ (accessed 1 September 2023).

Chapter 2

1. Abate, T. (2020). Black drivers get pulled over by police less at night when their race is obscured by "veil of darkness," Standford study finds. *Stanford News* (5 May). https://news.stanford.edu/2020/05/05/veil-darkness-reduces-racial-bias-traffic-stops/.
2. Trompenaars, F. and Hampden-Turner, C. (1998). *Riding the Waves of Culture.* New York: McGraw-Hill.
3. Simonson, A. (2022). A Black customer was awarded $4.4 million in damages in racial profiling lawsuit against Walmart. CNN (22 August). https://www.cnn.com/2022/08/22/us/black-customer-racial-profiling-walmart/index.html.
4. Kahneman, D. (2013). *Thinking Fast and Slow.* New York: Farrar, Straus and Giroux.

5. Gladwell, M. (2005). *Blink: The Power of Thinking Without Thinking*. New York: Back Bay Books.

6. Goethe, T.S. (2019). Bigotry encoded: Racial bias in technology. Reporter (2 March). https://reporter.rit.edu/tech/bigotry-encoded-racial-bias-technology.

7. Iyamah, J. (2023). 6 design failures that could have been avoided with inclusive UX research. User Interviews (8 June). https://www.userinterviews.com/blog/design-failure-examples-caused-by-bias-noninclusive-ux-research.

8. Akhtar, A. (2019). Artificial intelligence is slated to disrupt 4.5 million jobs for African Americans, who have a 10% greater likelihood of automation-based job loss than other workers. *Business Insider* (7 October). https://www.businessinsider.com/mckinsey-finds-black-men-will-lose-more-jobs-automation-2019-10.

9. Sawyer, W. and Wagner, P. (2020). Mass incarceration: The whole pie 2020. Prison Policy Initiative. Press release (24 March). https://www.prisonpolicy.org/factsheets/pie2020_allimages.pdf.

10. The Sentencing Project. (2018). Report to the United Nations on racial disparities in the U.S. criminal justice system (19 April). https://www.sentencingproject.org/reports/report-to-the-united-nations-on-racial-disparities-in-the-u-s-criminal-justice-system/.

11. Latino Decisions. (2012). How media stereotypes about Latinos fuel negative attitudes towards Latinos (18 September). https://latinodecisions.com/blog/how-media-stereotypes-about-latinos-fuel-negative-attitudes-towards-latinos/.

12. Muramatsu, N. and Chin, M.H. (2022). Battling structural racism against Asians in the United States: Call for public health to make the "invisible" visible. *Journal of Public Health Management Practices* 28 (Suppl 1): S3–S8. https://www.ncbi.nlm.nih.gov/pmc/articles/PMC8607736/.

13. Renée, L. (2018). Systemic bias vs implicit bias: Why the difference matters when reviewing the report by the Ontario Human Rights Commission on Racial Profiling by the Toronto Police Services. Medium (10 December). https://leesareneehall.medium.com/systemic-bias-vs-implicit-bias-why-the-difference-matters-when-reviewing-the-report-by-the-e2fdd8da6574.

14. Benson, A., Li, D., and Shue, K. (2022). Potential and the gender promotion gap summary (22 June). https://danielle-li.github.io/assets/docs/PotentialAndTheGenderPromotionGap.pdf.

Chapter 3

1. Shah Paikeday, T., Young, C.S., Sachar, H., and Stuart, A. (2019). A leader's guide: Finding and keeping your next chief diversity officer. Russell Reynolds

Notes **205**

(1 March) https://mcca.com/wp-content/uploads/2019/11/Chief-Diversity-Officer-Materials.pdf.

2. McCrae, R.R. and Costa, P.T. (1987). Validation of the five-factor model of personality across instruments and observers. *Journal of Personality and Social Psychology* 52 (1): 81–90. https://doi.org/10.1037/0022-3514.52.1.81.
3. Bennett, M.J. (1986). A developmental approach to training for intercultural sensitivity. *International Journal of Intercultural Relations* 10 (2): 179–195.
4. Hammer, M.R., Bennett, M.J., and Wiseman, R. (2003). Measuring intercultural sensitivity: The Intercultural Development Inventory. *International Journal of Intercultural Relations* 27 (4): 421–443. https://doi.org/10.1016/S0147-1767 (03)00032-4.
5. Hammer, M.R. (n.d.). The Intercultural Development Inventory, https://www.idiinventory.com/ (accessed: 1 September 2023).
6. Trompenaars F. and Hampden-Turner, C. (1998). *Riding the Waves of Culture*. New York: McGraw-Hill.
7. Hewlett, S.A., Luce, C.B., and West, C. (2005). Leadership in your midst: Tapping the hidden strengths of minority executives. *Harvard Business Review* (November). https://hbr.org/2005/11/leadership-in-your-midst-tapping-the-hidden-strengths-of-minority-executives.
8. Kochman, T. (1981). *Black and White Styles in Conflict*. Chicago: University of Chicago Press.
9. Pierce, C. (1970). Offensive mechanisms. In: The Black 70's (ed. F. Barbour). Boston: Porter Sargent, pp. 265–282.
10. Sue, D. W. (2016). *Race Talk and the Conspiracy of Silence: Understanding and Facilitating Difficult Dialogues on Race*. Hoboken, NJ: Wiley.
11. Poussaint, A. (2022). Microaggressions. Courageous Conversation (17 February). https://m.facebook.com/OfficialCourageousConversation/posts/5067777999909043/.
12. Unstoppable Performance Leaders. (n.d.). The state of burnout for women in the workplace, https://unstoppableperformanceleaders.com/the-state-of-burnout-for-women-in-the-workplace/ (accessed September 2023).
13. Zippia. (n.d.). Chief diversity officer demographics and statistics in the U.S. https://www.zippia.com/chief-diversity-officer-jobs/demographics/ (accessed 1 September 2023).

Chapter 4

1. Katz, J., Merrilees, C., Hoxmeier, J.C., and Motisi, M. (2017). White female bystanders' responses to a Black woman at risk for incapacitated sexual assault.

Psychology of Women Quarterly 41 (2): 273–285. https://doi.org/10.1177/ 0361684316689367.

2. Cornwell, E.Y. and Currit, A. (2016). Racial and social disparities in bystander support during medical emergencies on US streets. *American Journal of Public Health* 106 (6): 1049–1051.

3. Ray, R., Brown, M., Summers, E., et al. (2021). Bystander intervention on social media: Examining cyberbullying and reactions to systemic racism. Brookings (2 October). https://www.brookings.edu/articles/bystander-intervention-on-social-media-examining-cyberbullying-and-reactions-to-systemic-racism/ (accessed 1 September 2023).

4. Peters, W. (Producer). (1985). A class divided. *Frontline*. https://www.youtube .com/watch?v=1mcCLm_LwpE (accessed 1 September 2023).

5. Melaku, T.M., Beeman, A., Smith, D.G., and Johnson, W.B. (2020). Be a better ally. *Harvard Business Review* 98 (6): 135–139. https://hbr.org/2020/11/be-a-better-ally.

6. Kahn, W. (1990). Psychological conditions of personal engagement and disengagement at work. *Academy of Management Journal* 33 (4): 692–724. https:// www.jstor.org/stable/256287.

7. Appelbaum, N.P., Dow, A., Mazmanian, P.E., et al. (2016). The effects of power, leadership and psychological safety on resident event reporting. *Medical Education* 50 (3): 343–350. https://doi.org/10.1111/medu.12947.

8. Liu, Y. and Keller, R.T. (2021). How psychological safety impacts R&D project teams' performance. *Research Technology Management* 64 (2): 39–45. https:// doi.org/10.1080/08956308.2021.1863111.

9. Tsikudo, Y. (2023). The relationship between impostor phenomenon, psychological safety and work engagement. Dissertation thesis. The Chicago School of Professional Psychology. https://www.proquest.com/dissertations-theses/ relationship-between-impostor-phenomenon/docview/2832696787/se-2.

10. Bejerot, N. (1974). The six day war in Stockholm. *New Scientist* 61 (886): 486–487.

11. Trainer, D. (Director). (1989). The rowdy girls. *Designing Women* (Season 4, Episode 6, 30 October). Columbia Pictures Television.

Chapter 5

1. Mind Tools Content Team. (n.d.). French and Raven's five forms of power. Mindtools. https://www.mindtools.com/abwzix3/french-and-ravens-five-forms-of-power (accessed 1 September 2023).

2. Aragao, C. (2023). Gender pay gap in U.S. hasn't changed much in two decades. Pew Research Center (1 March). https://www.pewresearch.org/short-reads/2023/03/01/gender-pay-gap-facts/#:~:text=In%202022%2C%20women%20earned%20an,%2D%20and%20part%2Dtime%20workers (accessed September 2023).

3. LeanIn and McKinsey & Company. (2022). Women in the workplace 2022. Part 1: The state of the pipeline. https://leanin.org/women-in-the-workplace/2022/the-state-of-the-pipeline/.

4. U.S. Bureau of Labor Statistics. (2022). Occupation finder. https://www.bls.gov/ooh/occupation-finder.htm?pay=$80,000+or+more&education=&training=&newjobs=&growth=Faster+than+average&submit=GO.

5. Southern Poverty Law Center. (n.d.). White nationalist. https://www.splcenter.org/fighting-hate/extremist-files/ideology/white-nationalist (accessed 1 September 2023).

6. Blavity Inc. (2023). The power of the Black community: How brands can tap into $1.4 trillion in buying power (17 May). https://blavityinc.com/black-buying-power/.

7. Komick, L. (2023). Susan Rice roasted for claiming racism has cost the US $16 trillion. *New York Post* (13 April). https://nypost.com/2023/04/13/susan-rice-roasted-for-claiming-racism-has-cost-the-us-16-trillion/.

8. Olson, A. (2023). A small venture capital player becomes a symbol in the fight over corporate diversity policies, AP (20 September). https://apnews.com/article/fearless-fund-dei-lawsuit-affirmative-action-f6359b2c6596b3ca41111a55e77d20e6.

9. Hobson, M. (2014). Color blind or color brave? TED [Video]. https://www.ted.com/talks/mellody_hobson_color_blind_or_color_brave?language=en (accessed 1 September 2023).

10. Broom, M.F. and Klein, D.C. (1995). *Power: The Infinite Game*. Amherst, MA: HRD Press.

11. Hofstede, G. The 6-D Model of National Culture. https://geerthofstede.com/culture-geert-hofstede-gert-jan-hofstede/6d-model-of-national-culture/ (accessed 1 September 2023).

12. Trompenaars, F. and Hampden-Turner, C. (1998). *Riding the Waves of Culture*. New York: McGraw-Hill.

13. Oprah: After the Show. (2017). Oprah explains the difference between a career and a calling. The Oprah Winfrey Show (21 October). https://www.oprah.com/own-oprahshow/the-difference-between-a-career-and-a-calling-video.

14. McIntosh, P. (1989). White privilege: Unpacking the invisible knapsack. *Peace and Freedom Magazine* (July/August), 10–12.

Chapter 6

1. *Little Miss Muffet* (1805). Songs for the nursery. London: Darton and Clark (p. 45).
2. Cox, D., Navarro-Rivera, J., and Jones, R.P. (2016). Race, religion, and political affiliation of Americans' core social networks. PRRI. https://www.prri.org/research/poll-race-religion-politics-americans-social-networks/.
3. Filmsite. (n.d.). Filmsite movie review: The Birth of a Nation (1915). https://www.filmsite.org/birt.html (accessed 1 September 2023).
4. Durr M. and Wingfield, A.M.H. (2008). Keep your 'n' in check: African American women and the interactive effects of etiquette and emotional labor. *American Sociological Association* 37 (5): 557–571. http://doi.org/10.1177/0896920510380074.
5. Argyris, C. (1970). The Ladder of Inference.
6. Senge, P. (1990). *The Fifth Discipline: The Art and Practice of the Learning Organization*. New York: Doubleday/Currency.
7. Johnson, S.K. and Sy, S. (2016). Why aren't there more Asian Americans in leadership positions? *Harvard Business Review* (19 December).
8. Smith, W.A., Allen, W.R., and Danley, L.L. (2007). Assume the position . . . You fit the description: Campus racial climate and the psychoeducational experiences and racial battle fatigue among African American male college students. *American Behavioral Scientist* 51 (4): 551–578.
9. Owens, J. and Massey, D.S. (2011). Stereotype threat and college academic performance: A latent variables approach. *Social Science Research* 40 (1): 150–166.

Chapter 7

1. Schein, E.H. (2004). *Organizational Culture and Leadership*. San Francisco: Jossey-Bass.
2. Butera, A.C. (2001). Assimilation, pluralism and multiculturalism: The policy of racial/ethnic identity in America. *Buffalo Human Rights Law Review* 7 (1).
3. Gumperz, J. (1964). Hindi-Punjabi code-switching in Delhi. *Proceedings of the Ninth International Congress of Linguistics*, 1115–1124. The Hague: Mouton.
4. Hammer, M.R. (n.d.). The Intercultural Development Inventory. https://www.idiinventory.com/ (accessed 1 September 2023).

5. Mason, K. (2022). Study: Over 3 in 5 are hiding something from their employer. Job Sage (28 April). https://www.jobsage.com/blog/authenticity-in-the-workplace-survey/.

6. Collard, M. (2022). Bring your whole self: The value of authenticity. *Forbes* (28 November). https://www.forbes.com/sites/forbeshumanresourcescouncil/2022/11/23/bring-your-whole-self-the-value-of-authenticity/?sh=58f6429f53a6 (accessed 1 September 2023).

Chapter 8

1. MindTools Content Team. (n.d.). The Johari window. MindTools. https://www.mindtools.com/au7v71d/the-johari-window (accessed September 2023).

2. Argyris, C. (1970). The Ladder of Inference.

3. Senge, P. (1990). *The Fifth Discipline: The Art and Practice of the Learning Organization*. New York: Doubleday/Currency.

4. Bennett, M.J. (1986). A developmental approach to training for intercultural sensitivity. *International Journal of Intercultural Relations* 10 (2): 179–195.

5. Hammer, M.R., Bennett, M.J. and Wiseman, R. (2003). Measuring intercultural sensitivity: The Intercultural Development Inventory, *International Journal of Intercultural Relations* 27 (4): 421–443. https://doi.org/10.1016/S0147-1767(03)00032-4.

6. Hammer, M.R. (n.d.). The Intercultural Development Inventory. https://www.idiinventory.com/ (accessed 1 September 2023).

7. Trompenaars F. and Hampden-Turner, C. (1998). *Riding the Waves of Culture*. New York: McGraw-Hill.

8. Geert Hofstede (n.d.). The 6-D Model of National Culture. https://geerthofstede.com/culture-geert-hofstede-gert-jan-hofstede/6d-model-of-national-culture/ (accessed 1 September 2023).

9. Salovey, P. and Mayer, J.D. (1989/1990). Emotional intelligence. *Imagination, Cognition, and Personality* 9 (3): 185–211.

10. Goleman, D. (1995). *Emotional Intelligence*. New York: Bantam Books.

11. Dining in the Dark (n.d.). Dining in the Dark Chicago. https://dininginthedark-experience.com/chicago/#info (accessed 1 September 2023).

12. Parenti, C. (2021). The first privilege walk. Nonsite.org (18 November). https://nonsite.org/the-first-privilege-walk/.

Index

Page numbers followed by *f* refer to figures.